WHEN PUSH COMES TO SHOVE

RUGBY LEAGUE
THE PEOPLE'S GAME

Ian Clayton
Michael Steele

YORKSHIRE ART CIRCUS
1993

Published by **Yorkshire Art Circus**
School Lane, Glass Houghton, Castleford
West Yorkshire WF10 4QH
Telephone: (0977) 550401

© Text : Yorkshire Art Circus and contributing authors
© Cover Design : Tadpole Graphics
© Photographs : Michael Steele
Typesetting: Ian Daley at Art Circus Education
Printing: Thornton and Pearson Ltd.

ISBN 0 947780 98 X
Classification: Sport/Photography

Art Circus Support Team:
Reini Schühle, Ian Daley, Rachel Van Riel, Louise
Winfield, Pam Davenport, Steve Davenport, Olive
Fowler, Tony Lumb, Brian Lewis, Jill Brown

Yorkshire Art Circus is a unique book publisher. We
work to increase access to writing and publishing and to
develop new models of practice for arts in the
community.
For details of our full programme of workshops and our
current book list please write to the address above.

Yorkshire Art Circus is a registered charity No 1007443

We would like to thank the following organisations for their support towards this project:

Open Rugby Magazine, Rugby Leaguer Newspaper, BBC Radio Leeds, British Sky Broadcasting, the Parliamentary Rugby League Group

We would like to thank the following people who contributed to this book:

Colin Anderson
Bob Ashby
Trevor Bailey
Jimmy Banks
Sue Barlow
Debbie Beanland
Ruth Beck
Howard Bibb
Christoph Biermann
Peter Birchall
Derek Blackham
Paul Briers
Gerald Brookman
Lord Brooks of Tremorfa
Steve Brumby
Geoff Bullock
Chris Burton
Gary Carter
Brian Caswell
Roger 'Zak' Chalkley
Mary Charnock
Trevor Christian
Margaret Christian
Richard Clarkson
Ian Clough
Ray Connolly
John Cornwell
Sam Coulter
Lawrence Cunliffe M.P.
Ian Daley
Ken Davenport
Steve Davenport
Charles Davison
Trevor Delaney
Colin Dennis
Jim Dickenson
Brenda Dobek
M. G. Dooley
Dave Downs
Ron Dredge
The Earl of Swinton
John Etty
Karen Evans
Steve Evans

Gary Fitton
Geoff Fletcher
Trevor Foster
Pete Foy
Tom Frankland
Len Garbutt
Robert Gate
Dick Gillingham
David Goldthorp
Sid Gomersall
Harry Gration
Roger Green
Mick Griffiths
Trevor Griffiths
Dave Hadfield
Brian Hambling
Brett Hambling
Herbert Hambling
Neil Hanson
Norman Harris
Chris Heinitz
Eddie Hemmings
Gary Hetherington
Gordon Higgins
Dave Hinchliffe M.P.
Peter Hinchliffe
David Hobbs
Ray Hough
Kim Howells M.P.
Doug Hoyle M.P.
Donald Hunt
A. Hurstfield
Harry Jepson
Robert Jolley
Reg Jukes
Tom Keaveney
Moira Keaveney
Ben Kellett
Martin Kelner
Rev. Ed. Kessler
Phil Kitchin
Sharon Land
Fred Lavine
Brian Lewis

Fred Lindop
Maurice Lindsay
Geoff Lofthouse M.P.
Malcolm Lord
Lord Lucas of Chilworth
Tony Lumb
Steve Martin
Eric Martlew M.P.
Elsie Martlew
Melanie Mays
Bert McCarrick
Ian McCartney M.P.
Roger Moody
Claire Moorby
Mick Morgan
John J. Morris
Arthur Murray
Peter Murray
Terry Mullaney
Catherine Mullarkey
John Newlove
Terry O' Hara
David Oxley
Martin Oxley
Geoff Page
Heather Parkinson
Pat Parkinson
Phil Paver
Dave Peacock
Dave Peck
George Pieniazek
Margaret Pilkington
Cyril Poole
Sylvia Poole
Ian Proctor
Paul Quinn
H. O. Randles
Malcolm Reilly
Trevor Renney
Barry Rennison
Bev Risman
John Risman
Loggy Roberts
Philip Roberts

Emma Rosewarne
Sheila Scargill
Jackie Sheldon
John Sheridan
Alan Sherralt
Tommy Smales
Neville Smith
Ike Southward
Mike Stephenson
Roger Stott M.P.
Lynn Taylor
Gordon Tegg
R. H. Terretta
Dicky Thomas
David Thompson
Graham Thornton
Albert Tock
Mike Ulyatt
Steve Wagner
Trevor Wainwright
Mark Wallace
Colin Welland
Chris Westwood
Eleanor Westwood
MartinWestwood
Jimmy Williams
Maureen Williams
Dave Woods
Nick Woolf
Terry Wynn

Editorial Team:
Steve Brumby
Richard Clarkson
Ian Daley
Roger Green
Ben Kellett
Claire Moorby
Peter Murray
Heather Parkinson
Loggy Roberts
Lynn Taylor
Chris Westwood
Maureen Williams

Contents

Foreword   David Oxley   7

Introduction   David Hinchliffe M.P.   9

Fight the Good Fight   Ian Clayton   11

Part I
Hills of the North Rejoice   13

Part II
Abide With Me   65

Part III
Till We Have Built Jerusalem   123

List Of Plates   166

List of Subscribers   167

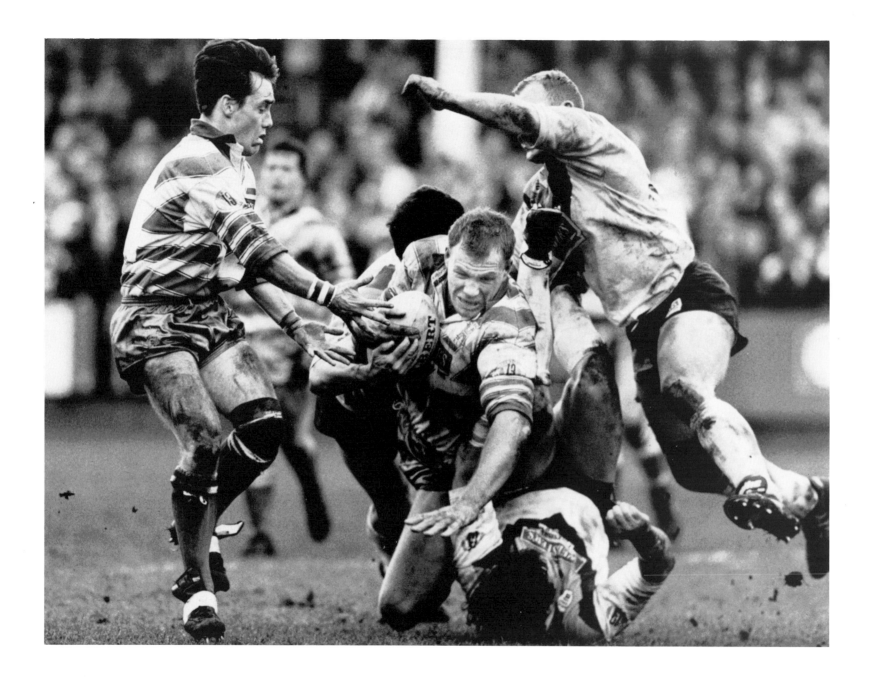

Foreword

'It's more than a game, it's a belief, a way of life.' This heartfelt testimony, so fervently expressed by one of the contributors to this lovely book, will be shared and endorsed by all readers whose communion with Rugby League dates from our earliest days and deepens down our advancing years.

Truly to know the great game, to understand the essential qualities which set it apart, is a precious gift. It is a life-enriching force, elevating the spirit and sweetening the soul. How lovingly is Rugby League's distinctive ethos expressed, explored and ennobled in the pages that follow.

Here are the committee-men and coaches; the kit-men and caterers; the referees, the administrators and all kinds of commentators. Here are the shrines where the faithful worship - Wembley and Wilderspool, Workington and Welfare Club. Here are the players, amateur and professional, with their characteristic courage, pride and humour, their down to earth honesty and easy approachability, so graphically captured by the fan who writes, 'You can put your arm round a Rugby League player and say, well done!'

At the very heart of the book are the inner thoughts and unshakeable beliefs of the fans, whose total identification with their heroes evokes a unique spirit of oneness, of belonging , thus creating a bond which transcends community to become communion.

'When I see Rugby League being well represented, it's a sweet feeling.'

This splendid volume will bring many a sweet feeling to all who love the finest of games and have good cause to bless its unique character.

David Oxley

Introduction

It is hard to explain to the unconverted how my own personal well-being for most of my life has been intimately tied up with the fortunes of Wakefield Trinity Rugby League Club and as a consequence, with the game in general.

Those who don't understand may gain a better idea of what I mean when they read this book. **When Push comes to Shove** is a unique celebration of the Rugby League community - the people who live and love the game. It is their own explanation of a passion for what some would say is far too modestly described as *The Greatest Game*.

From being a child, blessed with the privilege of being born into Rugby League country, I have also played, watched and loved the game, sharing in its many ups and downs. When a parliamentary colleague from Geordieland described me in a derogatory sort of a way as a 'one sport man', I pleaded guilty. I readily confessed to an abiding passion for a sport that to me offers everything - speed, personal courage, unbelievable skills, finesse and - on occasions - sheer brutality.

And I suppose I have always felt as well some political affinity with a game that emerged from the day to day struggles of working people in the industrial North and has suffered numerous attacks from the sporting establishment throughout its near one hundred year existence.

Like many of my era, I was banned from Rugby Union for committing the cardinal sin of playing amateur Rugby League after reaching the age of eighteen. As an M.P. many years later I have seen first hand how the prejudice against Rugby League remains alive and well at the most senior levels of government, civil service and the media.

Fighting this prejudice was one of the main reasons why - in the very room in which Cromwell signed the death warrant of Charles I in 1649 - the Parliamentary Rugby League Group was born in 1988. The group was encouraged to learn of the proposal to produce this book, with its novel approach to the recording of Rugby League's voices. We are delighted with the end result.

Having to spend much of each week nowadays in London, I share the frustration of many exiled northerners at the minimal media coverage of our game in the South. More than ever I feel genuinely sorry for the many millions in this country who are denied the greatest sporting spectacles. Ian Clayton, Michael Steele and their colleagues at Yorkshire Art Circus are to be congratulated for sharing with them through this book just a little of the marvellous world they are missing.

David Hinchliffe M.P.

Fight the Good Fight

'When the Rugby season starts', says Colin Welland in his contribution, 'I sit in the Metropolis and pine.' It's easy to see why.

Unashamed pride in place, environment and upbringing shines through in all the stories and images which make up this book. Rugby League goes beyond mere physical exercise - it means birthright, and opposition to an increasingly systemised world where everything is pigeon-holed and organised like a day out to the local theme park.

I was born at number 4 Mafeking Street, Featherstone. As a lad when I wrote my address I used to write 'Featherstone, near Pontefract.' As I grew older I realised that as many people had heard of Featherstone Rovers as had heard of Pontefract Cakes. Nowadays when I write my address I just put Featherstone. Rugby League has given me that pride.

Halfway down Mafeking Street, in a house under siege from cobwebs and rent collectors, lived Johnny Hope. Even my grandfather called him an old man, Johnny was that old. I liked to go and sit with Johnny in front of his fire while he spun bizarre yarns about his life, pausing only to spit gobstoppers of coal dust into a crackling fire. On hot days we'd sit on his front step and he'd pass brown hens' eggs to women walking by, an old man passing on wisdom or holy oval mascots. On cold days he'd warm his arse over the fire and like some mysterious soothsayer he'd breathe in and announce, 'In 1906 Featherstone Rovers beat Widnes in the second round of the Challenge Cup.' I knew what was coming next. Like a litany he would chant the names of all the Rovers heroes of that day: 'Randall, Higson, Jukes,' - 'Half of the terrible six', I'd leap in. And then on through, 'Kellett, Hoyle, Johnson,' just like a prayer.

That was twenty years ago. Three years ago I received a phone call from Christoph Biermann. 'Hello,' he said, 'I am a German sports journalist living in Bochum and a magazine called *Die Zeit* want me to do a piece on Rugby League. I wonder if you can help?' I put the phone down and thought about the boundless possibilities. If a man sitting with his tea on his knee in a former West Yorkshire coal mining town can have a conversation about Rugby League with a journalist sitting at his laptop computer in Bochum what other scenario might this game throw up? A splendid image. But then it's not surprising really with a game that is enjoyed with equal gusto in places as far flung as Papua New Guinea and Rochdale.

Complementing Christoph's article with his own images was photographer Michael Steele. We maintained contact and this book is the result. We wanted to show that the fans as well as the players and administrators have all got tales to tell about the greatest of all team games and how the environment has shaped it. At the beginning of last season Michael set about visiting every ground and I started collecting stories in all the Rugby League grounds. I wanted to delve into the rich heritage but also to find pointers to the future as the game approaches its centenary. The tales came flooding in. It was a heartache to select and edit.

There have been many memorable times in the year that it has taken to compile this book; Maurice Lindsay and Bob Ashby made efforts far and above the call of duty to help me. David Oxley made an excellent job of proofing and weeding out factual inaccuracies. I had a magnificent weekend in Cumbria as the guest of John Risman and family and at the Houses of Parliament as the guest of Ian McCartney, M.P. for Ashton-in-Makerfield. Sky Television's Sports Department allowed me to roam around their offices and interrupt the making of a *Boots and All* programme. And many players have taken time out after training to have a natter. Best of all, I have been talked to death and almost drowned in correspondence by hundreds of fans of Rugby League. It is to them that this book is dedicated.

Ian Clayton

Hills of the North Rejoice

A fist held high

Testimonials to the greatest game

☐ The scent of aromatic oils hangs heavy over the heads of the players and invades the senses. One after the other puts his hand into the container full of grease in the centre of the changing room, or pours oil over arms and legs. While the players put thick layers of Vaseline on their eyebrows and cheek bones they undergo a change. The grease is their war paint, the aromatic substances fire the excitement; now the miners, engineers and bricklayers turn into fighters.

The smile disappears from their faces, the jokes abate. Restlessly the long metal studs of their Rugby boots click on the tiled floor. The team captain sits bent over and coughs with excitement. Before his team members have time to realise that his cough is really a retching he gets up. His face is distorted as he barks into the room, a fist held high. Much of it is unintelligible but they all hear the most important bit, 'Knock 'em down!'

Finally the door opens abruptly. Outside the loudspeakers blare. There is a background murmur. The captain grabs the rugby ball and leads his team out into the cold of a northern English winter's day, out into the arena, out into eighty minutes of unrelenting battle.

> *Hills of the North, rejoice*
> *River and mountain-spring,*
> *Hark to the advent voice.*
> *Valley and lowland, sing:*
> *Though absent long, your Lord is nigh;*
> *He judgement brings and victory.*

☐ What you don't have, you don't miss. Familiarity breeds contempt. You don't value something until it's no longer there. All the cliches apply and I miss Rugby League sorely. On a regular basis, that is; top class Rugby, week in, week out. I've lived in London for thirty years and, save for the first four glorious seasons of Fulham when I was never away from the place (my wife said I popped down at lunchtime for a fix) I've been struggling to survive on a gruel diet of Rosslyn Park and Richmond's finest, starved of the greatest game in the world.

People say that of all games, don't they? But most from a basis of total ignorance of all others. This is particularly true of Americans who can elevate their stop-start affairs to world status simply because nobody else plays them. Most soccer aficionados have a mere fleeting knowledge of other codes, and Rugby Union supporters, secure as they are in the Barboured, if suffocating, embrace of the establishment, only occasionally glance beyond their barricades.

We Rugby League fans, bombarded by the massive media coverage afforded to other major sports, are uniquely positioned to make a sounder than most judgement. And we come down firmly on the side of Rugby League. It's not without faults - sometimes there's a sameness about its patterns of play, and scrums are a farce, and I'm worried about the ascending concentration on defence. But all these are more than outweighed by the exhilaration of total commitment, brave and fearless aggression given and taken, mind-blowing dexterity under

pressure, wit, extravagance and speed, all served up on a platter of discipline and total sportsmanship.

This is what I miss, this is what all other pursuits lack, this is what I've travelled half way around the world to see.

So I sit in the metropolis and pine, shooting up the M1 to sup at the fountain whenever time allows. I gaze enviously at the television pictures of Central Park, Headingley, Wilderspool and Knowsley Road and think, 'You lucky people! Satanic mills or not, you don't know you're born!'

□ My baptism came on a grey November afternoon in 1961 when, at the age of seven, I was offered an alternative to shopping with my mum and my sisters. The occasion remains one of my earliest, most vivid memories - a Yorkshire Cup Final between Leeds and Wakefield.

The fact that I managed to get lost in the sizeable Odsal crowd and finished up sheltering from the teeming rain underneath a policeman's cape only added to the sense of adventure. This was pure escapism, another world. The policeman and I eventually spotted my father.

I don't think anyone in my family could have possibly realised the all-consuming passion I would develop for the game, how it would shape my life entirely. Almost instantly, Rugby League gave everything a new meaning.

I soon began to yearn for the weekly escapism of going to the match, but it wasn't just watching the game which captivated me. It was everything that was attached to it in a schoolboy's mind - reading and collecting programmes, autograph hunting, the upkeep of my scrapbook and just the simple day-to-day process of being clued-up on what was happening.

By the age of eleven, Rugby League was such an integral part of my life that my weekly fix was an absolute necessity. At sixteen that fix needed to be fed more frequently than once per week.

Fortunately I was born at the right time to be able to over-indulge. The game's Sunday revolution was just starting and, with Leeds steadfastly refusing to budge from their Saturday fixtures, I was able to watch two matches on virtually every weekend throughout the 1970s. Thus, my ground-hopping, all-consuming passion for the game began in earnest.

Initially, I was devoted to one team, Leeds, and if the teenage years are your most impressionable I was fortunate to pay homage at Headingley during a period when Leeds played some magnificent football. Roy Francis's champagne side ensured that I was hooked for life on the joys of the 13-a-side code.

Interviewing the great man and discussing his career just before his death in 1989 proved to be one of the most treasured moments that my job has allowed me.

While Leeds remained my first love, their success gradually began to matter less and less. As I began to appreciate the struggles of clubs lower down the scale a genuine love of the game as a whole began to supersede that previous devotion to Leeds. Watching a variety of teams without having an emotional stake in the outcome of the game enabled me to appreciate the game for its own sake. But, equally, there is something uniquely uplifting about being brazenly, passionately involved in the proceedings. Seeing your team climb off the floor to win a Wembley Cup Final, as Leeds did in epic fashion against St. Helens in 1978, really is a sweet feeling.

Rugby League has enriched my life in so many ways. It has allowed me to travel the world to become friends with people I genuinely admired, to become acquainted with some fine, honest people right around the globe and to earn a good living as a journalist into the bargain.

□ Rugby League is the cream on top of my cake. It has lifted me up out of my council estate and enabled me to enjoy more of the pleasures

in life. I can get a car when I want one, a holiday, and I can give my kids and wife things that they want. Don't get me wrong, I'm not a snob or anything, but I am in a position to enjoy things. What it doesn't do is give you skills for the rest of your life. I want to come out of the game knowing there will be other things for me to do. I am still pleased to live in the town where I was born and to socialise with people I've always known, but there are one or two who still want to have a go. Because everybody knows you, you become a target. I have been careful where I've left my car because it's a club car and I've got my name on it.

☐ I'm very proud to be associated with this game. My line of business takes me all over the world and I leave a piece of Rugby wherever I go. I've left scarves in America and pennants in Korea. I'll tell you why I do it. It's because Rugby League is a much maligned game, because it's not recognised by the establishment. When I see Rugby League being well represented, it's a sweet feeling.

☐ When I watched *Another Bloody Sunday* and they put the action in slow motion to the music of Prokofiev, I was astounded. I thought then if you could choreograph this it would be breath taking, like ballet.

☐ I went to Grimethorpe to show some kids how to play Rugby. It's a rough coal-mining village. The kids were in a youth club, running about like lunatics while two youth leaders sat playing chess on £10 an hour, ignoring them. I chucked the kids a rugby ball and they loved it. At the end they all wanted to know, 'When's tha coming again, Fred?'

Rugby League is the finest game a young working class lad can ever play.

☐ It's not easy being ten thousand miles from my team. Sure, I still suffer the match-day blues and broodings, even though in this half of the globe kick-off time is when I'm asleep. The difference now is I get to suffer a whole lot longer. Relief doesn't come my way for two long days, since it's Tuesday when *The Australian* in its wisdom prints First Division Rugby League results from Britain. By Tuesdays, edgy doesn't do me justice. Do I open the paper quickly and risk spoiling the day early, or do I save it and spend another day pretending a win? I'm like a long-tailed cat in a room full of rocking chairs.

All this doesn't take into account mid-week and Friday night games, the scores of which are sometimes printed, sometimes not. This is not only downright inconvenient since it can be up to ten days before I hear of a score in these circumstances, it's also extremely dangerous.

That is a hell of a time for a long-tailed cat to be surrounded by rocking chairs.

Life isn't all sunshine, surf and *Sylvania Waters* here. Take the size of the spiders. If spiders had nicknames, these would be called Arnie. My wife, a blasé Aussie, will say, 'This one isn't poisonous. Shift it.' Of course it isn't poisonous, dear. When you're that big you don't need to be. You lot think it was just the Rugby League team that came in large sizes from Down Under. Don't you believe it.

So next time you're wondering why you put yourself through all the grief for that bunch of losers and wonder if it's all worthwhile, spare a thought for me and remember one thing - you're better off following a bunch of losers from where you are than I am following my bunch of losers from where I am.

☐ I was stationed in Germany in 1970. I will never forget scouring the English newspapers for the Rugby results and having no luck. Then I realised that all the papers over there were printed south of Doncaster and were not interested in what goes on outside London. After that I arranged for my mam to send over the *Pontefract and Castleford Express.*

Twenty odd years later my coach driving job takes me all over the country and I find nothing much has changed. No reports of games

if the paper is bought outside of the North, and you've no chance if your team is in the Second or Third Division. Sometimes you need a magnifying glass to find your result hidden away in small print next to the 0898 chatline adverts.

☐ *The Independent* newspaper was one of the best things that happened to Rugby League. For the first time the south of England got reports and results. *Open Rugby* has brought debates out into the open. Rugby League should pride itself on being a sport where everybody gets their chance to have a say.

The scales fell from my eyes
Being introduced to Rugby League

☐ It was the terraces at St. Helens that gave me my Damascus experience. It wasn't the first game of Rugby League I had ever seen, but it was possibly the first time I had watched Wigan, and at the height of their powers.

It was Easter Friday, 1992. Wigan had already won the Championship. They were looking forward to the Cup Final and had another league match on the Monday, so one might have expected them to be at less than full throttle. They started as if released from a pen. They seemed electrified. They simply flew at their opponents.

Two tries were scored quite soon and then, perhaps the fire cooled, but their defence never did. Every tackle had a match-saving intensity. One was made not just on the line but over it, the would-be scorer hauled back in mid drive. Not in any Rugby had I ever seen anyone being reverse framed like that. At another point the St. Helens wing broke clear and set sail for the corner, no one in his path. He had to score. But miraculously, two defenders got back and like aerial torpedoes put him in touch at the flag.

Wigan, it seemed, were set on zero-ising St. Helens. They were only 10 minutes away from doing that when an attempted counter-attack by Offiah let in St. Helens for their only try.

I was impressed, too, by the absence of a single retaliatory reaction by a Wigan player, not something I had ever seen demonstrated quite so clearly in Union. I had already been told by various players that 'You're a bigger man if you can ignore a cheap shot.' Seeing that kind of discipline on a field is another matter; and it did make their players, and their team, look superior.

At the same time there was a slight downside. There was a period in the game where part of me was still in awe of the unrelenting commitment, while another part of me was looking for something different to re-focus my attention. Also, my left ear drum was in danger of being perforated by the very shrill and hostile shouting of the young female next to me.

It is true that sometime later I told a friend that 'The scales have fallen from my eyes.' He seemed quite pleased to hear it. I won't go so far as to say I've been converted to League, but I don't think I'll ever get as excited by the sight of a Union forward ploughing 10 yards or so through a thicket of fellow forwards. The admiring cry from my T.V. set of 'A great drive there by the big lock' will, I'm afraid, fall on deaf ears.

☐ I was brought up in Liverpool and so soccer came first, but I was working for Radio 2 doing Rugby League commentary. One night Castleford were playing Hull in a semi-final replay at the same time as Liverpool were in the European Cup. I was thinking about being at Headingley where my job was instead of Anfield where my heart was, when an amazing thing happened. The Rugby League match started to take me over and totally swallowed me up. It was then I realised how great this game is.

☐ I was getting ready to go to bed one Sunday night '*Scrumdown*'s on', I heard my dad say to my brother, 'I was sitting there,' as he pointed at the exact spot on the screen. I decided to watch it a bit. I thought, 'But they're good looking!' I fully expected Rugby League players to have beer bellies and squashed faces.

When I got to my first game, I couldn't get over how the crowd reacted, talking and shouting all the time. At the end of the game I heard people saying, 'Well done, Paul. Well done, Gary,' and so I joined in saying well done and a big prop forward shook my hand. I was thrilled to bits on the way home. I thought, 'That's it, that's the game for me,' because these men are so approachable. Now I like it for all that and not for the good looking blokes with nice legs. You can put your arm round a Rugby League player and say, 'Well done!'

☐ It is more than a game, it's a belief, it's a way of life, it's a constant fight for justice, fairness and human rights. Those outside the game may find that to be crazy, but those in the know will understand.

As a teenager at college, I was banned from playing Rugby Union because I'd played League at the weekend. I see, even today, the problem that players have in France, where their jobs are threatened if they play Rugby League. My European Parliamentary colleagues can't believe the abuse that takes place against what is after all to them only a game.

☐ The Rugby Union and Rugby League comparison really frustrates me. I started to watch the England and France Rugby Union match the other Saturday and part way through I went out to do some gardening. I would never do that if a Rugby League Test Match was on.

☐ They tried to organise a contest between Rugby League and Rugby Union. Paul Docherty who was the Head of Sport at Granada Television made a proposal to the English Rugby Football Union. The idea was that Great Britain Rugby League would play England Rugby Union at Wembley. Forty minutes under League rules and forty minutes under Union ones. We expected to realise a million pounds which would have gone to the *Children in Need* charity. I understand the Rugby Football Union turned it down.

☐ Being born in Wales I've played Rugby Union from a very early age and loved every minute of it. When I first moved to England, the circle of friends I tagged on to were Rugby League fanatics. We spent many a drunken evening arguing the merits of our respective codes.

One Sunday morning they were short of a second row and they dragged me down to the dressing room, strapped me into a pair of

shoulder pads and threw me out onto the pitch. I was completely lost, I was like a baby in the jungle. After a while and a few embarrassing ball releases I settled in and started to enjoy it. I still remember to this day my first run. It was exhilarating. The scrum-half made a gap and tossed me the ball in open space, I was off and charging and never looked back. Since then I've played every time I've been picked and look forward to Sundays almost as much as Saturdays.

It is a great shame that the two codes don't get on, each could learn a lot from the other. I'm a much more complete player now and Rugby League could learn from my game, not least scrummaging. I have to do my fair share of extra pints and lethal cocktails on Saturday nights for the crime of playing Rugby League, but it's not a crime when I'm throwing dummies and charging for thirty yards or bring a man to the ground with a crunching tackle.

☐ We had been invited by the Southern Amateur Rugby League to compete in a sevens competition for the grand sounding Keith Macklin Trophy, matches to be played on Sunday morning following the Wembley Cup Final.

I had provisionally chosen the players for our two team entry, not on the basis of any game

plan but on sobriety and the knowledge of who would be fit enough just to be able to stand up. Our first team were named the Racehorses and a conglomeration of piss artists formed our second string, named the Carthorses.

The day dawned darkly that Sunday morning. Trying to ignore my own hangover I had the unenviable task of assembling the players, a morning spent pulling players out of bed or from under beds. Things were that desperate I resorted to holding up four fingers.

'How many can you see? Three.' - 'That's enough, you're in the first team.'

If they could get off the pot, they were picked. Finally the players were press-ganged, staggering and stinking, onto the team coach.

Hackney Marshes, the venue, contains a vast area of sports pitches. Unfortunately on our arrival there seemed to be no-one connected to Rugby League. Inside the reception area and changing rooms we were informed by the caretaker that he knew nothing about any sevens competition. In the true spirit of amateur Rugby League we left a message in chalk on the notice board: 'Lock Lane ARLFC been and gone to the nearest pub'.

It didn't take much booze to top up the previous night's indulgences and after an hour things were really beginning to swing. All thoughts of the seemingly aborted competition had disappeared into a plethora of silly grins and rugby songs. Suddenly, panic stations. The pub speaker system booming out the message, 'Is there a Yorkshire Rugby team in the pub, and if there is get to the competition immediately.'

All things considered, we didn't disgrace ourselves, although the southerners may have disagreed on this point. We did occasionally adhere to the rules and etiquette of orthodox Rugby.

The Racehorses galloped into the final and were narrowly beaten and the Carthorses covered themselves in mud and glory to win a secondary competition. We returned to Castleford with two magnificent trophies.

The following season we were requested by the event organisers to return the trophies but alas, we were not invited to compete.

□ In 1968 Normanton Grammar school from the West Riding of Yorkshire confounded all prophets by taking part in the Public School Seven-a-side competition at Roehampton and winning it! How could this be, that a school at the heart of a Yorkshire coalfield could beat the pride of Kent and Surrey, the might of Wales and the finest the Midlands could offer? Not so incredible really. The school's catchment area covered Castleford and had recently included Featherstone and Sharlston, two prolific producers of Rugby League talent, many of whom went on to be internationals. Here we had, entering the hotbed of Rugby Union, lads who had been born with a Rugby ball thrust into their hands before they could walk, lads who had played touch and pass on the local playing fields with their nappies still on. Add to this a PE teacher called Alan Jubb who had played for Wakefield Trinity and you have the ingredients. So good in fact was the recipe that not only did the school win the trophy that year, they went back and defended it successfully the year after.

□ I try, I really do try to like Rugby Union. Honest. I see it on the telly. I see fifteen likely lads stride out in the white, white and whiter than white of the motherland and I think, 'Crikey! Blimey! Go get 'em, Rory!' They kick, they chase. They kick some more, they chase some more. They create an overlap. They kick, they chase. Kicking and chasing. They push and shove. Pushing and shoving. They feel delighted with that down at Rosslyn Park. They change ends at half time. They kick, they chase. Kicking and chasing. They pack in their jobs as farmers and become high-flying city types. They have a line-out. They kick, they chase. Kicking and chasing. They are amateurs after all. They kick, they chase. Kicking and chasing. They aren't half boring.

A heart under a jersey
Playing the game

☐ Mal Reilly became a folk hero in Australia but he had problems with a niggling knee injury. A mate of mine once saw a big hoarding advertising a newspaper and on it it said, 'The knee' and everybody knew what it was about, Mal was that well-known.

☐ It's a good feeling when you connect. I can distinctly remember my first ever big hit. I was at Huddersfield and we had a pre-season friendly, First Team versus 'A' Team. I was up against David Jeanes and I found him running straight at me. I dropped my shoulder and knocked him straight down. A gush of air came rushing out of his body and I suppose I felt a bit bad at the time because he was already coming to the end of his career. But you never show it. It's all about facing off and respect. If someone is coming full pelt at you and you knock him onto his arse, it might make him think twice next time. If he comes at you again and again, you know then that he's got a big heart under his jersey.

☐ There are three ways a winger can take a ball, all of them on the run; you can run on to it, run in to it or run with it and that's when you go down the outside lane. Watch some of these wingers today and they're setting off from a standing start.

Coaches' systems have taken a lot of the individualism out of the game. We made signs to one another in my day, we often knew by instinct what our team mates wanted to do. Nowadays players go on the field equipped with a mental diagram of patterns of play. We didn't have tackling bags in training either: if you couldn't tackle you didn't play. We used to be attacking off our own line, that's why spectators came through the turnstiles. The slowest man or the fastest should be able to score from anywhere.

Even a carthorse can run when it gets going. It's knowing when to switch it on and off.

☐ I suppose Cumbria is the last bastion of parochialism. We tried to spread the game to East Cumbria by playing Carlisle's second team's home games at Penrith. I remember when Trevor Renney played. He was a Rugby Union player from the Cockermouth third team and on his first League run out he was up against the great John Atkinson, then in the twilight of his career. After ten minutes you couldn't recognise one player from another, it was hock deep in mud. Both captains asked for an abandonment but the ref.was determined to carry on. The ground slowly sank until the game was being played under water, the worst conditions ever seen. In the end they beat us with a team of fifteen-stone submarines.

☐ I was on a free transfer at Workington and training at Barrow. One of the lads came into the dressing room and told me that Fulham were starting a team. I'd never heard of anything like that. I was teaching at Salterbeck School at the time when Reggie Bowden phoned me up and asked me if I would sign on for Fulham.

'We want to try and develop the game in London,' he said. 'Come down and see us.'

I made my mind up before I put the phone down. A few days later I went to train at Golborne near Leigh. There were six of us; me, Reggie, Ian MacCorquodale, Derek Noonan, Roy Lester and Tony Karalius. By the second training session we were joined by big Ian Van Bellen and a few more, and soon we'd reached the magic figure of thirteen players. I believe Neil Tuffs was the thirteenth man to sign. We had great times. At the start we went to the local boozer and bought six rounds. By the time Tuffsy came we were on to thirteen rounds.

I have had plenty of highlights in my career, but that year was the best. Not only me thinks that. We played Wigan in the first game and over ten thousand people turned up to

watch. We beat them 24 - 5. We'd had no warm-up game, just promotional activities around London. That was a memorable day.

☐ I firmly believe, seeing as I helped to start it, that BARLA, the British Amateur Rugby League Association, has helped the whole game. We always argue that the professional game benefits from us amateurs both on the field and off, because when we create teams we also create spectators. It gave me no end of pleasure to see that sixteen out of the seventeen lads who beat Australia at Wembley a few seasons back had come from the amateur ranks.

☐ If your house is filled with your trophies then that's too much for a young lad to compete with, so when Wayne was about ten I took all mine down. You'll not see a trophy of mine on display in this house though I've won plenty in my time.

I also made sure that he wasn't pressurised into playing. When I set off to train the nine year olds my wife would say, 'Take him with you' and so I would but I let him play in the sand pit. Then one day I threw a ball to him and he threw it back. The week after he said, 'I think I'll play next time.' I said,' When you're ready, there's no rush.' That was twelve years ago and he now plays for Workington.

☐ Leeds tried to sign Jonathan Davies a long time before Widnes got him. I remember how I took him to his first match. He'd asked if he could bring his girlfriend up from Neath and I said he could. We booked them in at the Queen's Hotel as Mr. and Mrs. Carter. It was the middle of the week and he had to be back on the Saturday to play. He wanted to see a game and the only match on was a Yorkshire Cup replay at Post Office Road with Rovers and Hull K.R. I was worried for Jonathan because we were put in a big glass-sided box on show. He was calm about it. He said, 'They can't crucify me, I'm visiting a friend.'

We went in the boardroom after for a cup of tea and a bite to eat. All the pressmen were there; Wilson, Thomas, Richards, all the national press, and nobody recognised him. When Widnes signed him he was introduced at the Wigan and Widnes final at Bolton and the press swarmed him.

Lads who've been the backbone
After retiring

☐ It annoys me when I see Rugby League lads doing nothing after they retire. Far too many ex-players who are capable of going into administration are never given the opportunity.

You can gamble that a lot of the top profile jobs in Rugby League go to ex-Rugby Union men; Doyle-Davidson, David Watkins, Ray French, they've all done well, while the lads who have been the backbone don't get a chance.

When I was a lad in the 1950s I had a paper round. I used to take a paper to an old man in a wheelchair who had no legs. He always asked me, 'Are you behint?' If I said 'No' he would talk to me about Rugby and want to know how I was getting on in the school team. My dad told me that he was Anthony Starks and when I got older I found out that he was one of the most famous players who ever wore a Hull Kingston Rovers' shirt. Up until then he'd just been an old man with his legs blown off in the First World War and with his Rugby memories.

☐ When you finish playing Rugby League it's good to be able to put something back. Some go into coaching, some into administration and a few into media. Being in the media helps me not only to make a living, but also to keep in touch and digest new styles and methods.

When I first started I had no skills in broadcasting. The first thing I decided to do was lose my northern accent. I concentrated on saying things like 'running' and 'passing' instead of 'runnin' and 'passin'. That doesn't mean to say I have to have a plum in my mouth.

At one time it had been my entire dream to play for my country. I did that. I cannot go on living on that past glory. People have to be aware that there is life after Rugby League. Unfortunately some players can't accept that the accolades they get now finish when they stop playing. The wonderful present is not an everlasting gift, it is merely what you are now.

☐ I read in the papers today that Billy Banks had died. I was at work when I read the news. It would have been pointless of me to say, 'Do you know who's dead?' because my work mates wouldn't have had a clue who I was talking about, mainly due to the fact that most of them are female and the males too young to remember a great little half-back, even if they'd been interested in Rugby League in the first place. The obituary said that he was 66 years old, was a Welshman from Maesteg who 'came up north', signed for Wakefield Trinity, then moved to Huddersfield in 1948. It was while he played for Huddersfield that most of my generation will remember him best. He was number seven in the middle of an all-time great team that included Lionel Cooper, Mick Sullivan, Russ Pepperell, Johnny Hunter, Pat Devery and that great Scot, Dave Valentine.

My mind drifted back to the vision of a short sturdy body in a claret and gold jersey, breaking away from the scrum, his shock of brown wavy hair bobbing up and down over his forehead as he ran with the ball. He would then give it to 'Pepp' or produce his speciality, a neat little kick over the pack, to gain valuable yardage for his team.

My reminiscence, though, is personal because I once met Billy when I was a kid. We were living in Hunslet at the time and my dad was a professional handler of show dogs. The year must have been 1949 and I was twelve years old. A client of my father walked through the door one Sunday morning and who should walk in behind him but Billy Banks. Recognising him immediately, I was bowled over that such a star should walk into our little terraced house. Before he left I plucked up the courage to ask for his autograph and there, in my little blue book, I had his signature, scrawled in spidery writing, *W. Banks*.

I went to school the next day showing off my valuable treasure. For days afterwards I basked in the reflected glory of Billy Banks coming to our house.

☐ It's funny how many ex-Rugby League players end up becoming pub landlords. Sammy Lloyd made a go of The Minerva at the pier in Hull. Charlie Birdsall was in The Swan at Normanton last time I heard, and Brian Lockwood has had a few pubs. Perhaps breweries think they'll be good when it comes to chucking out.

☐ The funniest thing I ever saw happened at Nat Silcock's old pub The Royal in Hutchinson Street. Nat was in pain with his bad leg and hip from time to time. We regulars knew that and were fairly orderly when he was off sorts. One noisy character didn't heed the warning signs and got stroppy when Nat told him to behave or he'd throw him out.

'You couldn't do that in your pomp,' said the bloke to Nat.

Dead silence. Quick as lightning, one hand on the bar followed by a superb imitation of a flying elephant, over the top went Nat. You wouldn't believe so big a man could move so fast.

By the scruff of the neck and arse of the trousers, one awkward customer flew out of the door straight on to the roadway outside.

I really did think it was superfluous of Nat to add, 'And don't bother coming back, sonny.' You'd have thought Nat had scored a try at Wembley and kicked the winning goal, the applause he got. He even had a smile on his face.

'I like to keep an orderly pub,' he said. We heartily agreed.

The man with the golden mike in his hand

The commentators

☐ Picture the scene if you can. It's October 1990, the Australian second team have just beaten Wakefield Trinity convincingly. Three men have been sent off. Bobby Fulton, the Aussie coach, is being interviewed by his court of Australian reporters. Contrary to public belief, most of them are sycophantic in their approach and infuriating at best.

'The referee ought to have stayed at home where he belongs, with a cup of cocoa and his slippers on!' uttered Bobby to the nodding mass. Up steps the so-called genial host of *Look North*, self-confessed Rugby League fanatic with a diplomatic question.

'Don't you think your team lost control?'

He turned on me immediately and accused me of knowing little about Rugby League. I'm used to that, Wakefield Trinity fans accuse me of it all the time! I can accept it from them, but not from the likes of Bobby Fulton. The interview went round the world. In Australia it made front page news. A diplomatic incident had been created.

The feud between us continued for two years. Even in Australia he ignored me. Or perhaps I chose to avoid him. In October again, this time 1992, the feud ended. David Howes, the Rugby League answer to Henry Kissinger, took me by the hand and led me straight to Fulton. The Australian glared, shaped as if to land me a right cross to the jaw, and then shook my hand. 'You're a pommy bastard but let's kiss and make up.' We made up. I have never kissed Bobby Fulton.

☐ Trevor Kay is truly a commentator's commentator. Whenever Radio Leeds are in town and the man with the golden mike in his hand is in place, you are guaranteed a full-blooded encounter.

From the moment the crowd slowly begins to build up you can usually sense that there is going to be a cup tie atmosphere, whether it is glorious sunshine or driving rain.

There may have been one or two doubts during the week but it still comes as no surprise when it is announced that both teams are per programme. And then the teams run out, often to a tumultuous welcome while a lot of people are still making their way into the ground, which is a tradition among Rugby League supporters.

The hooter goes, the referee acknowledges the time keepers and the kick-off is imminent. The ball is booted deep into the opposition's half, and with ten seconds gone and the score locked at nil-nil it usually means it's time to go back to the studio. Meanwhile, it's nip and tuck early on, with both sets of forwards testing each other out. There is no quarter asked and none given.

From there the game can follow any number of patterns. It can be a bruising encounter littered with blood-curdling tackles. Or it could be a typical end-of-season clash. Perhaps an upset might be on the cards. For sure, the referee will have to stamp his authority on the game early on. Blows might be exchanged but there will be no substitute for pace. And no matter who runs out victors, we can be assured of one thing at the end of the day. Rugby League will be the real winner.

☐ Last year I was at Rochdale Hornets' reunion dinner when Alec Murphy told the following gem.

Apparently when Roy Haggerty was picked for England, he sat next to Garry Schofield on the plane over to Australia. Before landing you're expected to fill out a lot of forms. The immigration people were a bit pissed off when they found out they'd got two Garry Schofields; Haggerty had copied his sheet!

When Channel 10 interviewed him they got some very unconventional answers. When asked, 'Whereabouts in Britain do you live?' Roy replied, 'The top of Ellman Lane.'

I learnt very early in the game that writing about it can expose you to all sorts of hazards. When I spent two seasons reporting on Blackpool Borough in the 1970s I did all manner of inadvisable things - like training with the team and, when the 'A' team was desperately short, turning out for them.

What should have been the most memorable of those occasions though, I can hardly remember at all. It was the day that the 1978 Kangaroos were being welcomed to Britain at a reception at Headingley. They were sponsored in those days by Tooths KB Lager and there were mountains of the stuff around the place. Now this was the first tour with Frank Stanton in charge, so none of the players was drinking any; that task fell to the pressmen.

At the end of a long afternoon, someone remembered that Widnes 'A' were at home to Borough 'A' that very evening. It seemed like a good idea, so a few of us piled into a car with a few ice cold tubes for the journey. When I staggered out at Naughton Park, the unmistakable figure of Albert Fearnley, who was then manager of Borough, was pacing the car park. They were short; I'd have to play. Play? I couldn't even walk straight, but I somehow managed to get kitted up and onto the field. This wasn't the best night to be playing Widnes 'A'. The props were Jim Mills and

Brian Hogan, both coming back from injury or suspension, or some combination of the two.

My recollection of what happened on the field is Jim Mills picking me up in one big fist at the first scrum and telling me: 'Let's take it nice and steady, shall we.' The rest of the game is lost in the mists, but I'm fairly sure I took it nice and steady.

We were at The Watersheddings in November 1990 and I'm commentating on the Oldham - Widnes game for Greater Manchester Radio. One of the things I pride myself on is the research I do before every game. I like to be well prepared. I know all the players' recent histories, triumphs and indiscretions, names and home towns of the referee and touch judges.

You can imagine how flustered I was then, when the anchor man at the studio said, 'And now we're going over live to Malcolm Lord at The Watersheddings for full commentary on the Oldham - Widnes match,' and I was forced to reply,

'Well Rodney I'm not sure what's going on here. The players have taken the field wearing black arm bands and now they're lining up for a minute's silence. I'll have to hand back to the studio and in the meantime I'll try and find out for you who has died.'

As soon as I was off air I turned to my

wife panic stricken and asked, 'Who's died?'

She gave me one of her looks. 'Millions,'she replied, 'It's Remembrance Sunday.'

A tail swinging a cat
Positions of responsibility

The committee were sitting at the front. The microphone wasn't working. All the seats were taken. The bar was shut for the duration. The Chairman looked nervous. The heating was on full blast. All the windows were closed. The tobacco smoke would have worried Greenpeace. The committee started to disappear in the mist. There was a mumbling of discontent. The tension was mounting. The Chairman stood up to speak. Boredom set in. Someone at the back dropped a glass. There were apologies for absence. The fog thickened. The Secretary reported a poor season but-it-was-hoped-that-things-would-get-better-in-the-season-ahead. Rumours circulated that someone at the back had collapsed with heat exhaustion. Questions were taken from the floor. Someone wanted a window opening. Someone else didn't. There was a slanging match. There was a vote. The meeting came to a close. There was a stampede for the fresh evening air.

You never forget your first AGM.

☐ We had a situation in Rugby League where the tail was swinging the cat. As a governing body we were condemning members' clubs for being too parochial, but we were nothing more than a big members' club ourselves. The scenario was that Yorkshire and Lancashire took it in turns to provide the Chairman of the Rugby League. It seemed ridiculous that a top job should be run like a lottery. You want the best man for the job.

The best achievement Rugby League has made is to restructure its management; we have broken new ground and at the same time brought about continuity. Apart from an emergency period during the First War, I am now the Rugby League's longest serving Chairman.

David Oxley and I were a great team. I was a powerhouse, he used to say, and I've got plenty of energy. But I've got to admit I don't come over well as a front man. I'm no good in front of cameras and microphones. David Oxley articulated a lot of my energy. I suppose where I was aggressive he was Mr. Nice; he found it hard to say 'No'.

☐ We went to a Rugby League Development Officers' meeting. Ann Thompson is the Chair of the Women's League and she was looking round. It was all big leather chairs and big tables. Ann said to me, 'Isn't it intimidating?' We realised we were in a very male environment.

☐ The directors selected the teams when I was at Barrow. They met at the Monday night board meeting, and to get to know if you were selected for the weekend you just popped round to the platers' shop in the shipyard at 7.30 on a Tuesday morning where the team sheet would be up on the notice board. If you didn't work for Vickers you had to wait another twelve hours to find out at Tuesday night training. This meant that the general public knew the team before the players. Incidentally, one of the directors worked in the platers' shop.

It was said that if you lined all the first team players up on the touchline and sat the directors in the directors' box, only one director would be able to name all the players. For one, they didn't know all the identities and two, they were so old and had such poor eyesight they couldn't see that far. These people ran a football club and selected the teams.

This was borne out one pre-season trial match within the club, reds versus blues. On the blues side was the legendary Willie Horne, Great Britain stand off. In the dressing room after the match one director approached Willie and said, 'I think you showed a little promise this afternoon. Would you like to come and have six trial matches with us with a view to staying on?' Needless to say, the dressing room was in uproar.

☐ I've seen trainers act like spectators, shout, eff and blind, get too involved, yack on as if there wasn't a job to do and then, when I am telling the lads what should happen, saying 'I never saw that'. How could they? They saw it like a spectator, all emotion and no analysis; not knowing what had happened, having no way of showing how it had to be played. I like to think that my watching and self control paid off. I didn't get too excited, in fact they called me the Ice Man.

☐ When I became coach at Bradford, after being a player, I still tried to be one of the lads, but it didn't work. They need to know where they stand. It was little things at first. You'd go in a pub after training and you'd get, 'Oh no, they're not here, they're in the pub down the road.' I also found it hard to tell people who I'd played alongside for five years as a mate that I was dropping them out of the team in a particular week. It was similar to the situation we had at Featherstone. I got up at five o'clock and went to work at the pit with the same lads that I trained, played and socialised with. Every Thursday after training we'd go on the ale. If anybody said they didn't want to go it would be 'Oh what's up with you?' You felt obliged all the time. One thing moving to other clubs has done for me is enable me to make my own decisions.

□ Being Chief Executive is a proud post. It is a test of my administrative ability. Being Chair of Wigan was more of a test of my soul. At Wigan I was on an emotional roller-coaster that never seemed to go down, just up and up and up.

□ I always knew Jonathan Davies would give us the first chance to sign him. We'd been watching him you see. I once went down to see him play against Cardiff with Peter Fox. It poured down all the way to Neath. When we got there I said to Peter, 'There's no bugger here' and Neath isn't a big place. They'd called the game off for waterlogged pitch. It's a glamourous life being an administrator.

□ The two things I haven't enjoyed about being a committee man have been the constant battle against relegation and the players contract system. When we've been fighting relegation I'm almost too afraid to go to a match. You wake up on Monday mornings and you don't know how you'll get through the week.

I don't like arguing at the best of times, so when I've had a lot of people on at me I've often thought about packing it in. Now we're in the Second Division it's a lot more fun; I approach it with a much lighter heart. The contract system caused me heartache. I don't think many people knew what the hell they were doing. There was no precedent for it you see. For the first year or so players came in and held pistols at our heads.

□ I find it very embarrassing sometimes when I walk into the directors' room and somebody says 'Hello'. I've said hello to more people I don't know since I became a committee man than at any time in my life. Now I've been doing it for a few years I've found a lot of friendship and affinity building up. You get to know your opposite numbers and start to help one another. The wives of committee men are the ones who get landed with the hard work, they are always called upon to provide hospitality. My wife fell for doing the teas. She's only got one table cloth big enough to cover the boardroom table so she always has to wash it.

My favourite ground for hospitality is Workington: you've only to walk in and ask about Billy Iveson and you're welcomed with open arms. I like St. Helens, they're big-hearted, and Widnes are a fantastic lot, we always get on well there. The only trouble is we never seem to bloody win, so I suppose they can afford to be nice to us.

□ When the sin-bin rule first came out a scuffle between Charlie 'Muck Spreader' Birdsall of Rochdale and Paul Briers of Hunslet saw the referee's intervention and off they went for a ten minute cool down. As they were walking off the pitch Paul asked Charlie if they had been sent off. 'Yes' he said jokingly as the players were good friends. Paul went off to the dressing room and got in the bath. The Hunslet coach, Paul Daley, or the 'Angry Ant' as he was known among his players, came running into the dressing room and asked Paul what he was up too. The bathing player casually replied to his coach, 'I've been sent off and I'm going to the bar.' Daley shouted back at him 'You've been sinbinned you silly bugger, now get back on the field.'

It made my blood boil
A fan's eye view

□ It was the night of the first ever Rugby League game at the newly completed Don Valley Stadium. Sheffield Eagles were to play Wakefield Trinity. As you might expect at such an auspicious event there was the usual smattering of dignitaries there. Among them was Trinity supporting M.P; David Hinchliffe. That night Hinchy had gone along with a chap called Glyn Robinson, a local trade union official. The

38

previous day Wakefield had announced the signing of Nick Du Toit, a South African player. The news that a South African had signed for Wakefield caused a bit of nervous concern for our two Socialists who spent the entire period before the game discussing the rights and wrongs of the issue. Anyway, the teams ran out onto the pitch and Glyn and David nervously scanned the Trinity team to see if they could spot any unusual faces, but as anyone who has visited Don Valley will testify the pitch is some considerable distance from the stand. Almost as a reaction to this Glyn says to David, 'I wonder if that South African bastard is playing?', at which point a rather large chap who had been sitting in the seat in front of them all along turned round and said, 'Nah, I'm not, mate.'

☐ I like to go watch Bramley. It's a small club in a small community which has been swamped by a larger one, consequently its inhabitants cling to their identity fiercely and it's this spirit which helps the Rugby League club cling to life against the odds.

There's corrugated sheeting missing from the roof of the covered terracing, bits of perimeter fence fall off if you touch it and often more people in the bar drinking under the stand than watching the game, even when it's not raining.

There's always plenty of local lads in the Bramley side as you would expect and the crowd never seem to get on a player's back if he makes a mistake. They are realists at Bramley.

A couple of seasons back I went to see Bramley play Nottingham City, who then as now were gallant easybeats. Maurice Bamford had taken up residence as coach and that added interest. Maurice is folksy but a bit frightening as well. He didn't so much as sit in the dugout as hold court there.

As you would expect, Bramley started to score plenty of tries. I'd positioned myself near the dugout so that I could hear and see what Maurice Bamford was saying and doing. People of his experience and stature see and understand things which even the most seasoned Rugby League fan would miss.

My attention was drawn to the behaviour of the sand boy, who, like many of the Bramley dugout retinue, seemed in awe of their leader. He kept trying to pluck up courage to tell Maurice something, but kept putting it off. I recall a similar feeling when I'd spilt Jusoda down the front of my check Whitsuntide shirt when I was a kid.

Finally the kid marshalled all the bottle within his being and spoke to Maurice: 'Maurice!'

' What?... Marquis (Marquis Charles, a rather distracted looking winger, now with Dewsbury) for Christ's sake get your slack self involved!...What?'

'I'm running out of sand'. He showed Maurice the bucket with only a few pathetic crumbs in it, as if he wouldn't believe him.

'Well, grind some bleeding rocks together then!'

The kid ran off as if the entire Kray family was after him.

A while later he came back looking all relieved, Bramley scored another forty points and it was all hunky dory in the sand department. Now I know Maurice is a good motivator.

☐ Wally Lewis and Wakefield Trinity were like poached salmon and pickled onions, the most outrageous mismatch of the century. But Wakefield had the money and that's why Wally was here.

I went to see him play a few times at Belle Vue and marvelled at his skill and feel for the game, and it was always a great disappointment to see his magnificent 30 yard passes bungled by wingers who were totally unprepared, stood with their hands on their hips and tongues out in awe of the master.

It was a big talking point in the game at the time, was Wally's salary, and a great side show to his games was seeing big forwards chase him round the pitch and thump him at every opportunity, to make him pay every penny back in blood.

One classic story of such an encounter is of Wally after several hard tackles, fists and kicks, was blatantly fouled in front of the referee. Wally opened his arms in astonishment at the ref's 'Play-on' decision.

'What have they got to do, ref?' said Wally pleading for mercy.

'What do you expect Wally, at a thousand pound a match?' replied the ref.

☐ You know when the Rugby team comes into the bar. They like to start shouting and singing. Then they get the big glass stein off the shelf and break raw eggs into it. I think the record is seventeen raw eggs topped up with a litre and half of Guinness. The lad who did it went straight to the lavatory to spew up. A Canadian lad who plays for Cockermouth Rugby Union club swallowed twelve raw eggs down and never flinched.

☐ There is a former Great Britain international second row forward whose name I won't mention. He had an incredible party piece. He would put old pennies down behind his foreskin. I think his record was 2/3d in old money.

☐ The spectators at Doncaster are a fantastic bunch. I finished my career there in the fifties and they really treated the players like royalty. The team was a second team playing amongst first teams. It was a mix of young lads trying to make a name for themselves and us old ones after a few more coppers. We always tried but were often outclassed. The fans turned up every week though and if we won the flags would go out through Doncaster. I'd always find something in my boot as well.

☐ The most daunting place I have to play is Featherstone. The ground's so compact that the crowd's right on top of you. They don't even have to shout if they want to hurl an insult. Luckily their accent is so thick I can never understand a word they are saying.

☐ I can't go to Headingley, or should I say 'Bass Headingley' to please the corporate sponsors, without wanting to spit. It's not the club I want to spit at nor the people of Leeds, not the players or staff, but the memory I have of an exchange of conversation between two middle aged Leeds fans who stood behind me at the famous ground in 1992. Some young Featherstone lads were barking and rawping and cheering on their favourites in a noisy and, I've got to admit, slightly aggressive way. Then I heard the couple say it. The lady, who was dressed in a fur coat and matching hat, turned to her partner and said, 'Ignore them, George, they're miners and they don't know any better coming from where they do.' It made my blood boil and the image is as vivid now as I'm writing this tale, as it was at the time it happened.

☐ Travel east or west on the M62 on Sundays and what will you see? You will see two stone pyramids bearing the white and red roses of the two arch rivals. You will see lots of Asian families in minibuses travelling to visit their relatives. You will see countless bridges and carriageways being repaired. During the miners' strike you would have seen convoys of Black Marias full of policemen being bussed to the coalfields. But go on it every Sunday between September and May and you will see the scarves, pennants and rugby jerseys of every Rugby League playing town in the country. The M62 is truly the Rugby fans' motorway.

☐ Perhaps the most memorable game in Blackpool's history, apart from their Players Cup Final appearance, was the day they won at Headingley in the First Division. With a friend I travelled to the match by train. Upon our return to Leeds railway station after the match we were greeted by the ticket collector who glanced

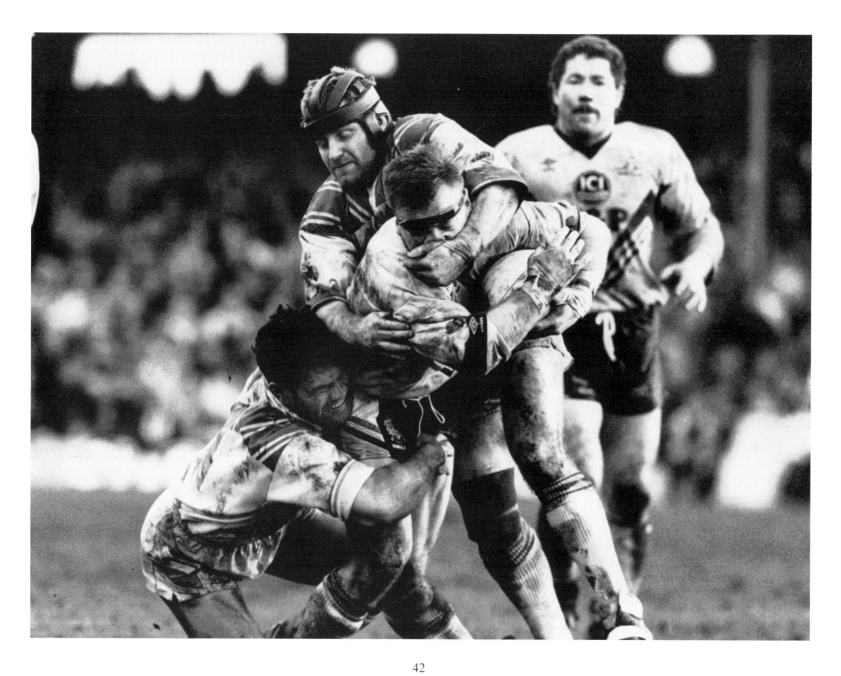

casually at our destination on the tickets and the following conversation ensued :

'Had a nice day lads?'

'Yes.'

'Did you win?'

'Yes.'

A long pause.

'You mean you won?'

'Yes.'

'You mean Blackpool Borough won?'

'Yes.'

'You mean Leeds didn't win?'

'Yes.'

'You mean Blackpool Borough beat Leeds?'

'Yes.'

'Bloody hell!'

At this point he disappeared from the barrier into the office and rushed around telling all and sundry that Leeds had lost. Meanwhile the queue of would-be passengers grew more and more restless behind us. Eventually he returned and let us through with the remark that he was a Hunslet fan and could not wait to gloat over all 'these Loiner fans that work here'.

☐ Sometimes incidents on the terraces are far more entertaining than the match itself. During the miners' strike in 1984, Castleford fielded a black-leg. Whenever this player approached anywhere near the touchline my mate took the opportunity to scream out 'Scab, Scab, Scab!' Sometimes this entailed him running almost full length of the field alongside the player. In the end the strike breaker lost his cool and lunged over the touchline fencing. The wind-up worked wonderfully.

☐ Blackpool Borough moved a couple of times following their ground safety problems at Borough Park at the end of the 1986/87 season. They eventually arrived at the home of Altrincham FC, Moss Lane, playing under the banner of Trafford Borough.

In February 1990, Trafford drew Warrington away in the first round of the Challenge Cup. Allan Sherratt, then Secretary of the club, suggested that Trafford use the game to promote their club in some fashion so that when Warrington were not playing or were playing away, their spectators might go to Trafford to watch a match.

Sherratt suggested that the club inflate twenty balls which had been especially produced with the club's name and logo on and get the Trafford players to kick them into the crowd as a public relations exercise. The players entered the field of play at Wilderspool to be met by around four and a half thousand spectators. They jogged to the four corners of the ground and proceeded to kick the balls into the crowd. Sherratt knew that his idea to attract the ardent Wire fans was immediately doomed to failure as the crowd proceeded to throw the balls back!

☐ There we were watching Trinity thrash about helplessly at Odsal yet again and the Wakefield supporters were well into moan mode. It was everybody's fault: Toppo had to go, the Board had to be sacked, it was all Mark Conway's fault (even though he wasn't playing!) and it was cold. Then, in a rare moment of subdued mumbling, came the comment of the evening. From the middle of the dispirited Trinity hordes came a lone voice, 'Do you know' the voice asked us collectively, 'it's like standing with a load of Victor Meldrews!'

☐ Doncaster were followed by two fanatical women who worked at a library and went everywhere to watch their team. At the time Doncaster were having a bad spell and it all came to a head when they were getting beaten easily at Chiswick by Fulham. The two librarians, Caroline and her mate Mary, were there. The Doncaster winger, Audley Pennant, got tackled right on the touchline in front of the two librarians.

'Oh, get up Audley, for goodness sake!' shouts Caroline. 'I could lay on the grass with a gang of men on top of me.' There was a hush in the crowd, everybody looked round and then for Caroline the realisation dawned.

☐ We were playing at Whitehaven one week. Our team had just scored a try and the Whitehaven players were grouped behind the posts. They included the very famous Norman Lofthouse, a man without a hair on his head. Someone from the crowd shouted, 'Ayup Norman, why don't you get two rabbits tattooed on your head?'

'What you on about?' Norman shouted back.

'Because from here they might look like hares.'

☐ When Kemble and Leuluai and O'Hara first came over from New Zealand, Hull were playing Castleford on a really freezing cold night. I'd gone with Gordon Fishwick, and our wives wanted some Oxo to warm them up. We were sat in the stand so they had to pass the cups of Oxo and hot dogs down the row. My hands were cold and I didn't get hold of the plastic cup properly, I spilled it into Gordon's lap, he squeezed his bread roll and his sausage shot down a Cas fan's neck. He turned round rolling his sleeves up. Luckily he saw the funny side of it.

☐ The weirdest supporters Hornets have got must be the Birmingham Four. Every weekend they make a round trip of at least 200 miles. They used to follow the Solihull Barons ice hockey team, but got fed up with it so they looked to Rugby League and found Hornets at the bottom of the first division. They reckon it took six months to discover we weren't called 'Rochdale Hornets nil.'

☐ My first wife used to come to all the matches with me. I was refereeing York and Hunslet and as usual I got her a ticket then settled her down in the directors' box.

Driving home after the match I said, 'Did you enjoy it?'

'Well it was a bit embarrassing...'

Whatever could she mean?

'Embarrassing! What do you mean embarrassing?' I asked.

'Well, I got talking to a smashing friendly couple, but she said, 'I've never seen you here before.' So I said, 'No I'm only here for the day.'

'You with the St. Helens party?'

'Like I said I'm only here for the day.'

I couldn't stand it any longer. 'Why didn't you tell them you were with the referee?'

'You must be joking,' she replied. 'They were playing hell about you.'

☐ During the late 60s and early 70s, banners were all the rage at Rugby matches. In fact they were so popular at one stage that you couldn't go to a match anywhere without seeing at least three or four, whereas now you only see them at major cup finals or Test Matches. I had one myself, a piece of best bottom bedsheet stretched between two six-foot bamboo poles; my pride and joy, that banner was. I took it to all the games, in fact it even went to Whitehaven without me when I was poorly.

The funniest banner I ever saw, though, was at Batley, I think it was a cup tie. The banner belonged to two Batley lads who were eagerly awaiting the arrival of their heroes. As kick-off time approached, the Rovers took to the field, followed closely by the Batley side who have the nickname of 'The Gallant Youths'. As they ran out, the two lads unfurled the banner with great ceremonial aplomb to reveal the legend, 'Batley The Gallant Yoths.'

☐ When we went on a coach to the World Cup Final at Wembley, I was sat next to my best mate Richard. There was a huge model of the world on the pitch and a lot of people in the ground and suddenly the world burst open and loads of balloons went into the air. A cannon went off, there was a buzz in the crowd when the players came out and they started to chant.

We went ahead two-nil, the Aussies came back, but we had a half-time lead of six-four. With ten minutes to go, the Aussies scored a try but after that I thought we'd scored. I started dancing around with Richard, nothing mattered but the try. Then I sat down as Richard said to me, 'Oh! they knocked on'. Martin Offiah walked off the pitch in a sulk. I can't tell you what the man standing behind me said.

☐ Programmes. It's all a matter of programmes. Cumbria versus anybody are the hardest of all programmes to get hold of. Be honest, when was the last time you saw one on *The Antiques Roadshow*? That just shows how priceless they are. People have been known to pawn their grannies just to add a 1985 Cumbria versus New Zealand to their collections. Cumbria County programmes are rarer than a break by a Great Britain forward, harder to get hold of than Terry Lamb's jock strap.

Consequently all the Rugby League programme collectors worth their salt descended on Barrow on the night Cumbria played the Aussies, just to get their mitts on the hottest investment since British Gas shares. There were folk from all over - Fulham, Westhoughton, even Keighley. At least forty five percent of the crowd that night had come just for the programmes, and blow the game!

One lad from Wigan - don't they talk funny - was really worried. He had heard that the Aussie games at Halifax and Oldham were all ticket and all the tickets had gone. How was he going to get the programmes? None of the other collectors cared as long as they got some.

As we stood around waiting for the programme sellers to appear, a huge Rolls Royce drove up to the main entrance. Naturally we thought they must be delivering the programmes - but no. Out stepped a lady of mature years and ample proportions all buttoned up, if fur coats button up, against the cruel Cumbrian climate. Of course we were all gobstruck. Lady programme sellers arriving in Rolls Royces, they were certainly doing the Aussies proud!

Eventually she approached our group, greeted us cheerily and took us somewhat by surprise by pointing to her chest area and saying 'I bet you don't know what's under here lads.' Well there were a few knowing glances exchanged and then there followed a surge forward by the bulk of the group, most of whom thought that she meant the programmes, others merely having carnal thoughts. It was all too much for the Wigan bloke who turned puce and hurried away into the murk.

We were all hugely disappointed when the lady's coat was unbuttoned. There were no programmes, no visible female charms, just a golden mayoral chain. She was only the Mayor of Barrow-in-Furness. However, she had one redeeming feature - she came from Huddersfield originally and consequently talked proper. She talked big as well. She said that if we didn't get hold of a programme we only had to write to the Mayor's Parlour and she'd make sure we got one. Obviously she didn't know what she was on about.

Anyhow, we did eventually get a programme. Mission accomplished. Now, if anyone out there has a copy of Cumbria versus New Zealand 1985, I'll swop my granny for it.

☐ I have read a lot of books about Rugby League from Rothman's book of statistics to Geoffrey Moorhouse's richly textured essays. Without a doubt the finest book I've ever read on the game is the Minute Book of the Featherstone Miners' Welfare. It is pure social history, but not a boring academic tome, a book of social history written by the people who make it. From making arrangements for Santa's visit to the Christmas party, to arguments about who should pay for the scrum half's broken front teeth, from raffles outside Hillard's supermarket to raise money for the trip to play in Paris, to stern condemnations of the brawl after the annual players' dinner, this book has got the lot.

And if your cylinder water heater element ever needs moving further down the tank, the Miners' Welfare know an NCB engineer who can do it!

☐ The piece of memorabilia I prize is my Uncle Dan Frawley's Australian touring blazer from 1905. Balls, boats, boomerangs - I've got the lot. My attic is a shrine to Rugby League. I show my collection all over and have raised thousands for charity. When you think of the stuff I've got it is amazing how little has been stolen. The only thing I can think of is an Australian pennant. We'd set everything out, people had been looking at the collection when it was time to show a film. When it was over my daughter said that the pennant was missing.

'Lock the door,' shouted Spanky McFarland, 'We are now going to switch off the lights so that the culprit can return the missing object. It's best that it is done this way because God help the person who has it if we have to do a search.'

With that the lights went out. We never got it back. It's reckoned that it was pinched by three young kids who left just before the film came on.

☐ There must be no end of people who wake up the morning after an auction in the social club wearing a bobble hat and scarf, remember how much they had to pay for it and think, what the bloody hell am I doing? We always do the auction last when everybody's tanked up. Manny Cousins once paid a thousand pound for summat daft, but I've known Joe Public pay up to 300 quid for somebody's Great Britain shirt.

It all started at the Willows Club in Salford after we came back from the 1975 World Cup. Jim Mills sang for Wales, somebody strummed a guitar for Australia and I did a comic spot. It was the first time I'd been on stage. Then we had the idea of doing a Rugby League Roadshow. The first one was for Paul Rose and a lot of stuff had been brought for raffles. We decided to auction it instead and it went from there.

☐ I was the first Pom to make a breakthrough in the Aussie media. I own my own marketing and PR company. I also own what is possibly the world's biggest private collection of Rugby League memorabilia; shirts, photos, programmes, medals. We put it all on exhibition on a train we called the Rugby League Express. The collection took up four carriages and we toured it around Australia over 20,000 kilometres. We took fold-down display cabinets into shopping centres and department stores and attracted great sponsorship. It was a big success, over a quarter of a million people came through the train.

☐ I don't like the Rugby League Hall of Fame at Oulton. Don't get me wrong, they've got some good stuff, but it's just as though it's been plonked down there for no other reason. And you can't really enjoy looking at the things on show when people are sat eating their dinners.

It's much nicer to visit pubs that are in Rugby League heartlands, like Billy Boston's at Wigan, the Railway at Featherstone, or the Market House at Dewsbury, places where you can truly see the connection between the game and its environment, where you're just as likely to look at a photo of Rugby League players and then see them in real life joining in with the karaoke instead of looking at a shirt in a glass case that reflects someone munching on a basket meal.

He's only got a broken ankle
Rugby League's characters

☐ When Keith Hudson was the groundsman at Doncaster, Dave Sampson was coaching. One night Dave wanted the lads to go and play touch rugby at Hexthorpe Plant Works athletic track. Dean Carrol asked Keith how to get there from Tattersfield. Keith said, 'Turn left, turn right at the roundabout, take the next right, the next left, straight on, right at the lights and you can't miss it.' Dean didn't take it all in, so he asked again.

'Oh, just follow your nose!' says Keith.

'I can't,' says Dean. 'Graham Idle's driving.'

Now anybody who knows Graham Idle will know that his nose goes in about seventeen different directions.

☐ I've been the Hornets timekeeper from 1984 and a fan since 1953. We were over in Dewsbury in 1988 and half-time was looming. The timekeeper was also the tannoy man whose duty it was to announce the scorers from his microphone. The hooter was one of them electronic jobs, not a hand horn like the rest of us use. When time came he pressed the hooter. Nothing! Pressed it again, still nothing. Then quick as a flash he grabbed the microphone with volume full on and did the best impression of a foghorn I've ever heard. It really reverberated around the ground.

I can still picture the look of shock on that referee's face and recall both teams looking our way with disbelief. You've never heard anything like it. Every time I meet this man we have a good laugh about it.

☐ Rugby League is not all glamour. I once watched a bloke at Bramley with a bucket and shovel getting dog shit off the field after a car boot sale. He must have spent half an hour doing it until the fans started coming in and then he stopped. I don't blame him. You're bound to get a bit self-conscious doing jobs like that!

Another time, I'd gone with the 'A' team and after the match we went to sample their corporate hospitality. A cup of tea and a Swiss roll about as far through as a beer mat. Bill Farrington said, 'You want to keep the bloody bacon slicer away from the Swiss rolls.'

☐ An old man told me that there are two things you need to be a good groundsman: at least 20 years' service and a sense of humour. You can get qualifications but I've never bothered. When I first started I asked if I could go on a course at Askham Agricultural College near York, but one of the committee men said, 'Tha'll get thi papers and then tha'll be off,' so I never went. As a result of that I've learnt everything I know by picking the brains of other groundsmen. When I first came here all I did was roll the pitch with a two ton roller and an old Massey Ferguson tractor. I thought, 'If it's flat they can play on it.' I rolled and rolled for five years, but the ground used to get very muddy. When I came to clean the boots on Monday mornings I had to fish for them in a pile of mud. Then Raymond Wright, who's the groundsman at Silcoates School told me I was compacting the pitch too much and spiking was more important to allow better drainage, that and light rolling. The pitch drains well now. The drains here are like a fish's back, herringbone they call it, one main channel down the middle and others running diagonally into it.

As for sense of humour; well, you need that because you get very little money and very little praise. At the end of each season they have awards for: best young player, best coach, best referee and I think they have one for best secretary now, but none for groundsman. All I get is 'There's a funny smell in the dressing room' on training nights. I've got more bosses than enough, I've got the committee, the players, the sports ground inspectors and every Sunday about 3000 spectators ready to have a go.

There are the perks though. I might get to Wembley once in a blue moon and now and again another club comes and you might hear somebody neutral say 'That's a nice field to play on.' That's worth more than money.

☐ As soon as the match is over I throw all the kit into three plastic dustbins full of cold water. While they're steeping, I swill the towels and jock straps in the sink. I have at least three strips to wash every week and that's a two day job. I started off with Persil but the committee thought it was too expensive so they went to Netto's supermarket and got me some called Yetza; I'm like Jesus feeding the five thousand with that

stuff, it only costs a quid a box but they expect it to go as far as Persil.

I have a system with boots. First I scrape the mud off with a knife, then I wire-brush them and wash them with a cloth and last of all put the dubbing on. The kitman I admire the most of all without a doubt is the lad at Bradford. He's the best bloke in the business: they play in white and they come out like snowdrops. Best groundsman for a laugh is Ocker at Warrington. He has a stable type door and he just leans on it smoking and taking the mickey.

□ Sunday, 12th November 1989 and we went to Belle Vue to see Trinity play Castleford. With us was Castleford-supporting Wakefield District Councillor, Trevor Kenworthy. During the pre-match imbibing big Trev was full of tales about what his hero, Rambo Gibbs, was going to do to the Trinity players. Imagine his surprise when the game had only just started and Gibbs caught a knee to the head and spent the next half an hour staggering around the field senseless. Our mate Trevor did have something to cheer about right on half-time when Rambo flopped over for a try after taking a pass from Southernwood. Alas, that was the last we were to see of Gibbs, on the pitch that is, as he didn't come out for the second half. Trinity won the game 22 - 14 and it was into the bar for a drink.

All this excitement had made Councillor Kenworthy rather hungry so he took advantage of Trinity's then exotic catering facilities and went to get some pie and peas. After about ten minutes of holding his pint I went to see where he had gone. I was just in time to see him emerge from a scrum of players with a steaming tray of green mush in one hand. As he came out of the melee he came face to face with his hero, Rambo Ron. Ron looked at Trevor and then at his tray of pie and peas.

'What's food like, mate?' asked Ronnie and, without waiting for Trevor to answer, stuck his finger through the peas and into the middle of his pie, twisted it round, pulled it out and sucked it.

'Mmmm, not bad,' were the last words Rambo Gibbs ever said to Councillor Kenworthy, who was stood there totally gob-smacked. We didn't laugh - much!

□ I got a trial for Bradford in 1950 and I travelled down with a lot of ex-Hull players who played for out of town teams. Some of them played for Batley and were having a run out in the Batley 'A' team, the team I was to face. Amongst them were two former Hull stars who had been transferred - Sid Hattersley and Bob Kavannagh. We travelled to the match together and as I went on to the pitch on this autumn day

they both came up to me, shook my hand and wished me all the best for the match.

In those days there were never any subs, so if anyone got injured the side was a player down. The famous saying amongst players was, if you hit someone, make sure he gets taken off.

The match had been going half an hour when the scrum half said he was going blindside, which meant I would automatically follow him, and when we won the scrum I broke blindside. That's all I remember of the game. I woke up on the dressing room table with the taste of sponge in my mouth. I said, 'What happened?' and the coach replied, 'Bob Kavannagh short armed you.'

Four of my bottom teeth had gone through my bottom lip, my nose was swollen and I had black eyes. I was dazed from the blow, but went into the clubhouse anyway. As I entered the club room, which was full of players, directors and supporters drinking and discussing the match, Bob Kavannagh came up to me and said in a friendly manner, 'I'll buy you a pint, Bri.' Through my damaged mouth I said, 'How the hell can I drink a pint?' He turned and said jokingly, 'I'll get you a straw!'

□ Rugby League players know all about the risk of injury and a lot of them approach it with a very unusual sense of humour. West Hull

Amateurs were playing and Pete Jordon took the ball in. There was a massive impact and Pete came out of it with his shin bone sticking through his sock. Somebody shouted to Billy McBride to send for an ambulance and he went round asking if anybody had ten pence for the bloody telephone.

Mick Crane had a spell at Hull K.R and there was a young winger there whose normal job was at the DHSS. Mick got a nasty bang and the winger was helping to carry him off with Mick's arms round his shoulders. As they got to the touchline, Mick says to the winger, 'Have you got any claims forms?'

☐ Arnie Walker was only a l'aal 'un but this forward hit him hard. He wasn't the first to go down that afternoon but I knew from the way he fell that it was a severe injury. As he lay there I was sure that he was dead. They fetched the ambulance on to the field; his neck was broken.

We were well in the lead but the match was abandoned with only ten minutes to go. Arnie recovered. He was nicknamed 'Boxer' Walker.

☐ I was coach and Billy Rhodes, one of the great characters of the game, was trainer. We were at Dewsbury and Alan Hardisty was the captain of our team. I was sat at the side of the field on the bench with Billy when Alan Hardisty went down injured. Billy brought him off and played about with his ankle. He rubbed it and strapped it and sent him back on. After about five minutes Billy turned round to me and said, 'He's got a broken ankle y'know 'as Hardisty.'

I said, 'Get him off quick!'

That was typical Billy!

☐ I have played against some of the greatest wingers ever to dance down the field of play. Peter Henderson was a former New Zealand sprint champion who would race around defenders using the full width of the field. Billy Boston would try a straight path to the goal line using his great strength to carry him forward. He had a wonderful understanding with Dave Bolton, his stand off, who would turn his back to oncoming defenders before parting with the ball. Brian Bevan was an elusive runner and a gentleman. He scored many tries by following up kicks and was never sent off for foul play in a long career. Tom Van Vollenhoven, St. Helens' South African, had explosive pace off the mark and Stan McCormack was the interception king. One of the hardest men was Eric Batten who would run straight at his opponents, legs and arms moving. He had a great understanding with his centre, Ernie Ward. Trinity's Aussie winger, Denis Booker once tried to jump over me and I'm six feet tall. Result, a bruise like a football on my chest. No wonder jumping over men was banned!

☐ In 1947 I had the honour of meeting Richard Auty, the son of a Batley mill owner and also the English Rugby Union fly half. He taught me how to do a double side-step. In 1960 I used this attacking ploy when playing for Wakefield Trinity in the Cup semi-final at Odsal. A long time to wait, but worth it.

I moved off my right foot to go to the left of the tacklers and, just as they came to nail me, I moved off the left foot to go right of them, reached over the line and put the ball down with one hand. Marvellous.

☐ Geoff Fletcher was a player who always led by example and never shirked a tackle. The memory of Geoff which I won't forget was after he had finished playing and was general manager at Runcorn. Hornets were there on a bitter cold day in January 1990. There was hardly anyone in the seats as it was still early but I saw a father and son who came from Rochdale. The father was in his seventies and had bad health but was keen as mustard for the Hornets and, as he sat huddled in his seat, I said, 'How are you Joe?'

'Bloody cold!' replied old Joe Hesketh. At this same instant Geoff Fletcher was passing and overheard.

'Who's bloody cold?' he asked, then seeing Joe, said, 'We can't have this.' Minutes later he returned with a huge whisky in a classy glass and almost bowed to Joe. 'Get that down you my friend and all the best.'

I don't know what put the glow in Joe's cheeks more - the whisky or Geoff's kind treatment. There's one thing I've noticed in all my years of timekeeping. The harder the man on the field, the gentler and more big hearted off it.

☐ One of the best players of the last fifteen years or so has been John Woods. He started off his career with Leigh but has also played for Warrington, Bradford and Rochdale, breaking records at these clubs, before returning to Leigh to finish off his career.

During his spell at Bradford he scored 36 points in one game, breaking the club record. He always liked a pint or two, and after this match he had something to celebrate in the players' bar at Odsal. On this occasion he perhaps had a few pints too many, considering he had to drive the forty-odd miles back to Leigh. He set off and chanced his arm. He picked up the M62 and was cruising along merrily at about 80-85 miles per hour, humming gently to himself, when he saw the dreaded flashing blue light approaching rapidly behind him. John thought this was certain to be the time when he was going to lose his licence. The police car caught up with John as he reduced his speed and came up alongside him. The two police officers motioned to our hero to pull over to the hard shoulder. John pulled up, got out of the car and walked over to the officers. One of them reached into his pocket, John feared the dreaded breathalyser. 'Would you please sign my autograph book', were the first words the policeman uttered. 'What a great game you had today.' An unusual opening gambit. Usually it's 'Blow in this bag, sir.'

It turned out that the two policemen were lifelong fans of Bradford, who'd been at the match that afternoon and seen Woodie's wondrous display. They merely wanted to congratulate him and get his autograph. However, it did teach John a lesson. No matter how many points he scored, or records he broke, from then on he stayed on shandies or got a lift back home.

☐ Unlike their soccer counterparts, Rugby League professionals have never been, apart from a few notable exceptions nowadays, what you might call prima donnas. The part time nature of the sport has perhaps guaranteed that paid Rugby League players never overreach themselves or entirely forget their roots in the community. For example, could you imagine the following scene I witnessed sometime in the 1970s, were it a sulking soccer star that I was describing?

An old banger pulls up mid-afternoon in downtown Featherstone. To my astonishment, our hero at the wheel is none other than the then Great Britain loose forward, who shuffles to the nearest off-licence. Replenishing his wine cellar perhaps? In need of a claret for the cheese and wine opening of his latest boutique? Not quite.

For he immediately emerges with a bottle of milk in each hand and in the dozen or so yards to his car he smilingly acknowledges several locals who have been pleased to cross his path. Most of his attention, however, is reserved for a couple of pensioners who have obviously seen him grow from childhood. As they engage him in an animated conversation they are clearly unperturbed by his footwear. Perhaps I was suffering from culture shock, or perhaps it was simply a matter of my high expectations of how an international sportsman should conduct himself in public being severely shattered. Whatever it was, I remembered thinking at the time that I couldn't have imagined Kevin Keegan or George Best nipping down to the corner shop for two pints of milk, wearing his battered carpet slippers!

☐ One of the famous Rovers stars of the past was notorious for not attending training sessions and equally famous for his far fetched excuses. He got away with it all the time and he knew the team coach couldn't afford to drop him. Probably his most outrageous excuse was the time a team mate rang his house prior to a training session to see if he would be going that evening. 'Oh! I'm sorry,' explained his wife 'he can't come tonight, he is going to concrete the driveway.' Well nothing wrong with that you might think, except it was the middle of December, snowing and dark at 4 o'clock.

☐ There's no doubt that Rugby League is the funniest sport in the world. One thing you will never get over is the humour in the game. I was over at Wigan recently; Shaun Edwards has bought himself a new black Mercedes. The lads in the dressing room are kidding him to death. 'What's up Edwards, haven't you got any funerals on this morning?' They say when he puts a cassette in the stereo it plays the Funeral March.

☐ Paul Medley is well known for closing his eyes when he comes to catch a ball in a difficult situation. In the Boxing Day match between Bradford and Halifax, Karl Fairbank dropped the ball in a collision, a Halifax player picked it up, ran off and scored. Peter Fox jumped up out of the dugout and shouted, 'Medley, you useless...!,' at which point Paul Medley, who was sat at the side of Foxy in the dugout said, 'It's not my fault Peter, I'm sat here with you.' Quick as a flash Foxy replied, 'Well you would have done that if you'd been on the field.'

☐ Bill Riches was my centre partner and good friend. On the way back from a game in Lancashire we stopped at a pub and Bill suggested a darts competition.

'We'll all have three darts, throw a tanner in the pot and the highest score takes the money.'

A clean ashtray was procured to hold the sixpences. Bill announced he would go last and everybody else started throwing. Then it came to Bill's turn. He threw the highest score by far, maybe even the maximum of 180, and then announced that he was the Hull Brewery darts champion!

☐ Jimmy Banks was a great scrum-half. He played for all the top amateur sides and signed pro terms with Doncaster.

He once went on tour with the Miners' Welfare to Paris and on the first day there he got lost. He told me that on the way back from the bar he turned right instead of left and missed his hotel. He walked about Paris all night, unable to speak a word of French. He was too frightened to ask directions and in any case, he didn't know the name of his hotel so it wouldn't have been much use. He found himself in the red light district, footsore and confused. Somebody gave him a bed for the night and the next day after a bun and a coffee he set off again. In vain he walked up and down streets hoping to bump into one of his team mates. No luck. Then, with blisters the size of tangerines on his feet, he staggered into the cool sanctuary of a cathedral. A young woman was playing the organ. He stood next to her and smiled as she finished her piece. It turned out that she spoke English. Jimmy explained his troubles and in response the young organist directed him to the British Embassy.

Twenty four hours, and as many miles of foot slogging after he first went missing, Jimmy approached the reception desk in the British Embassy in Paris.

'Can I help you, sir?'

'Yes. My name's Jimmy Banks and I'm over with the Miners' Welfare Rugby League team, and, and ...'

'Yes, sir?'

'Well, to tell thi't truth, I'm lost.'

They asked him if he knew the name of the hotel. He didn't. Did he know the street? He didn't. Did he know the district? He didn't. In the end they asked him if he knew the telephone number for the Progressive Club (that was the Miners' Welfare HQ), as they might know the hotel. He didn't know that either, but he did know the number for the Green Lane Working Men's Club nearby. Perhaps they would help?

The Embassy phoned the Green Lane Club, 'Hello. This is the British Embassy in Paris. Have you ...?'

'Bugger off!' The phone went down.

The Embassy worker persisted and phoned again. This time she got a more sympathetic hearing.

'Do you have the number for the Progressive Club?'

Now think about this. Sitting in a room in the Embassy in Paris, steeping his feet in a bowl of salty hot water is a miner from Ackton Hall Colliery. Waiting on the telephone is a young woman Embassy worker who has never heard of Ackton Hall Pit and is even less likely to have heard of its Rugby League team. Meanwhile, in the smoke-filled Green Lane Club, a committee man is walking about trying to get some information believing he has been asked for the latest Pigeon Club forecast numbers.

Of course the number the Embassy woman later called was useless. Things were not looking bright for our Jimmy. It looked as though the Embassy would have to repatriate one of its citizens.

Cometh the hour, cometh the men. The Miners' Welfare bus pulled up outside the Embassy. They had come for the boy, they had a game to play in an hour and Jimmy was on the team sheet. They burst his blisters, bandaged his feet, shoe-horned his boots on and onto the field our hero trotted.

They say that number one in the pop charts at the time was Bonnie Tyler singing *Lost in France*. They say Jimmy Banks got the Man of the Match award that day. They say the Embassy woman now follows Featherstone Rovers avidly. And the concert room in the Green Lane Club has the fragrance of March violets ...

Abide With Me

The Great North Road
Going to Wembley

☐ My dad's brother and sister never married. They lived together in the same house well into their eighties; each had habits which annoyed the other.

On the morning of my sister's wedding my aunt was so upset by my uncle that she forgot to put her teeth in and didn't realise until she was posing for the full group photo. Then she gurned a vicious scowl in my uncle's direction!

He had on his old gaberdine mac together with his Leeds Rugby League scarf and knitted bobble hat. I think he stopped short of bringing his rattle!

If the wedding had been anywhere near the date of the Rugby League Cup Final at Wembley I expect he'd have had his gaberdine mac decorated like a Christmas tree. He collected embroidered Yorkshire rose badges, silk bannerettes, and many other material items relating to the Leeds team: all these he attached with giant safety-pins to his mac.

It didn't matter whether or not his team was playing at Wembley - each year he went without fail, each year he decked himself in all his 'finery'. For several days before, during and after the Final he would wear this outfit.

*Abide with me, fast falls
the Eventide,
The darkness deepens,
Lord with me abide,
When other helpers fail,
and comforts flee,
Help of the helpless, oh,
abide with me!
Swift to its close ebbs out
life's little day:
Earth's joys grown dim, its
glories pass away;
Change and decay in all
around I see,
O thou, who changest not,
abide with me!*

Over a period of three years in the 1960s my sister and I were given a taste of Cup Final fever. I was studying sculpture in London and my uncle had the 'brilliant' idea of bringing my sister each year for the Cup Final, staying at my flat and taking me along with them.

I must say, with hindsight, I did enjoy the experience but never looked forward to the day. I lived in Muswell Hill which in those days was fairly quiet respectable suburbia. The residents weren't used to seeing fanatical northern Rugby supporters so close up but my uncle was oblivious to his surroundings. My sister and I were at the age when we could be embarrassed by the behaviour or dress of a companion. Neither of us was a fanatical follower of any sport so we felt a bit like fish out of water ... until, that is, we took our first steps up Wembley Way.

Then we saw hundreds of supporters equally fanatical as my uncle, all heading in the same direction. We were gripped by the mood and couldn't wait to get to our place on the terraces. The play was always exciting and with brief explanation of the rules by my uncle, we understood and enjoyed it all the more. We soon found ourselves cheering and jeering with the best of 'em. The atmosphere was always good - there seemed to be a happy family-outing feel to it all. I was safe in that crowd.

☐ I first went to Wembley in 1959. I took a job with British Rail on the buffet cars. I thought I was doing really well when I got the London run on Wembley morning. When we arrived in London the steward said we had to check the stock. The train pulled out to some sidings near Teddington. I thought, 'Oh no! I'm going miles from Wembley.' We did the stock check and the steward took me to one side and said, 'Right, go on then.' And when I looked I could see the two towers.

☐ We used to go to Wembley every year, whoever was playing. Before the motorways it was eight hours by bus from Hull. We always stopped at the Kingsley Hotel, Bloomsbury way. In 1980 when Hull played Hull K.R. somebody put a sign up on the old A63 out of Hull which said, 'Will the last person out of Hull please switch the lights off.'

☐ Wembley 1948. On our bus journey to the stadium we were caught up in a traffic jam and were running late. The driver was in a state of panic: could have been something to do with him not being sure of the route through London.

That great character, Frank Whitcombe, took over the driver's seat and proceeded to by-pass all traffic in front and put his foot on the pedals. We sailed through the centre of the big city, past the Houses of Parliament with motorists bellowing and waving fists at our bus. Frank, with his huge smile, sailed away to get us to Wembley bang on time. No nervous tension for this man prior to turning out at Wembley Stadium, and in fact Frank was named the Lance Todd Trophy Man of the Match, the first time a player on the losing side received this award.

☐ As a nation we are moaners. In Rugby League we seem to have more than our fair share. All a lot of people want to do is knock you down and hold you there. I like to get up and play the ball, then knock them back. I like the challenge.

I've come from a rank outsider to be Chairman of my chosen sport. From a not-good amateur who thought his crowning achievement was to trot out for Ackworth in the Challenge Cup first round proper at Wakefield Trinity, to walking out of the tunnel at Wembley leading the procession.

I've met some great people - Lord Gormley, Douglas Bader and them, but I never could get through *Abide With Me*. I get to the end of the first line, then I've gone.

☐ Because of the success of big games at Old Trafford and Wembley, we've started taking credit card bookings. We run two phone lines at the box office now. The tickets for Wembley arrive in February or March and by May we've sold over 70,000. If you had a stadium and you had to please everybody, they'd all want to be on the half-way line. I can't do it: it's first come, first served.

When we played the Test Match at Old Trafford in 1986, I sold a man some tickets and he got stuck in a traffic jam. He phoned me up on the Monday and said, 'You'll have noticed I wasn't there, can I have a refund?' They must think I've got nothing better to do. Mind you, I've noticed when I go to Wembley I miss a lot of the colour and atmosphere because I'm looking round to see if all the seats are taken.

☐ Since childhood the Great North Road has always fascinated me from the moment I first heard its name from my father. He said, 'It's four hundred miles long and stretches across two countries, joining their two capitals together.' In my boy's eyes I had visions of Buckingham Palace and Edinburgh Castle reaching out their long arms and joining hands at Ferrybridge where I fell under its spell.

Later at school I learned that Dick Turpin had ridden his horse from London to York along my very own road and I determined that one day I would emulate that amazing feat. Little did I know it would be another fifty years before I was able to make this dream come true. My steed was called Champion. It was red and had come from Korea and had cost me £25. It had ten gears, a pair of pedals and two wheels. Everyone said I was mad to cycle two hundred miles just to see a Rugby match, but it wasn't just any match. It was my very own Classy Cas playing Hull K.R. in the 1986 Challenge Cup Final at Wembley Stadium and hadn't a Knottingley clairvoyant seen Castleford players carrying a large silver cup?

I set off on the Friday after work, stopping at a roadside snack bar and stoking up with tea and toast. Two lorry drivers busy scoffing hamburgers were fascinated with my black and amber tracksuit and woolly hat. They nearly choked on their burgers when I told them where I was heading. I was soon on my way again on the hard shoulder of the Great North Road with their good advice ringing in my ears. I was feeling elated, the sun was shining and the miles were ticking steadily by. I crossed the River Trent at Newark. It was 3.30pm so I was making good time. Towards evening I was feeling rather weary and by 9.30 it was pitch dark. I had no lights so I sought bed and breakfast at a small village called Stilton.

'Is this the place where the cheese comes from?' I asked the landlord.

'It is indeed, sir. Would you like some?'

My fellow guests were all long distance lorry drivers and I got lots of advice on how to get to Wembley.

Next morning, full of bacon, egg and good spirit, I set off on the second leg of my journey. By 8am I had 95 miles to cover in seven hours. I made good progress until I reached Boldock. Then my troubles began. Because of roadworks I had to make a detour. The road got quieter and quieter and narrower and narrower. I was lost. I didn't know whether to turn back or carry on in the hope of rejoining the Great North Road further on. I carried on and was passing through a very pretty village with a duck pond and thatched cottages when the heavens opened. It began to rain and hailstones as big as marbles began to hit my face and body. It was now 11.30am and I still had a long way to go. I passed through a village called Sandy. 'That's an omen,' I said to myself. 'He's playing on the right wing for Cas.'

I stopped for some tea at another roadside snack bar and looked at my watch. Panic! 'How far is it to Wembley, mate?' I croaked at the proprietor. 'About ten miles,' he answered. I cursed, it was ten past two. I had fifty minutes to cover ten miles and I was tired out. I jumped on my bike and pumped the pedals like a man demented. The miles flew by as I overtook queues of traffic. Suddenly on the horizon I saw

a flag. The flag was on top of a tower. One mile further on I could see two towers. I threw my woolly hat in the air - the twin towers of Wembley were in sight. Ten minutes to kick off. I sped past the cars and coaches, zig-zagging through the late comers hurrying to the ground. I jumped off my bike like a rodeo rider and chained it to a fence in front of a bemused policeman. I ran all the way round the stadium looking for my entrance. I jogged up the hundreds of stairs, my breath coming in short rasping gasps. I found my E27 gate, showed my ticket and pushed my way along the rows of cheering, colourful spectators to my appointed seat and collapsed exhausted.

A whistle sounded in my ears. I looked at my watch, it was 3 o'clock. I looked on to the field as the ball sailed through the air for the kick off. The rest is just history. Castleford scored three stunning tries. The first by Tony Marchant, the second by Beardsmore and the third winning try by, guess who - Sandy of course.

☐ One of the best nights out I've ever had in my life was after Hull drew with Widnes at Wembley and replayed at Elland Road. I went with our lass. Widnes was a good team and I think young Lee Crooks was only eighteen. They were still letting people in at half time. We

won 18 - 9 and when we got back we went to the Red Lion on Clarence Street. Gordon was dancing about with a big sombrero on that he'd fetched back from his holidays. I don't think we came out until the milkman was coming round.

☐ My first visit to Wembley was with three hundred other schoolboys. They put us on a train at Paragon Station and we slept in bunk beds on the tube stations like they did in the war. On the Friday night we were taken to see Jo Stafford at the London Palladium and we spent the rest of the night scrapping and pillow fighting.

☐ It was on the eve of the Cup Final and you couldn't have got one more person into Craven Cottage. Over twenty thousand people. We beat Bradford 16 - 0 in a special challenge and a player called Dave Allen scored four times. We were on £375 to win that match and £350 if we lost. I believe Bradford were on £100 to win and £50 the loss. The day after the game all the Fulham players and their wives flew out to Portugal for a holiday.

☐ Learning to separate my emotions from professionalism is a skill I've acquired over the years. When Widnes beat us in the Final in 1984 I was dumbstruck. I could hear the band playing *Congratulations* and I saw the Widnes players clapping each other on the back as they did their lap of honour. Kevin Tamati came over, whacked me over the head and said, 'Don't worry mate, you'll be back.' Then Eric Hughes, the Widnes captain, came over. He was holding the big shiny cup decorated with black and white ribbons and said, 'It's got to you, hasn't it?' I nodded. 'When you come again, make sure it doesn't get to you.' I was upset for me and for my dad who'd gone to Wembley done up in my John Player blazer.

We beat Hull in that memorable Final the very next year. I talked to David Stephenson, our centre, who's a very rational lad. We decided that Wembley is just eighty minutes on a piece of grass - all that happens is you win or lose. All the players were told to block out their emotions for that eighty minutes. The game was the work and after that they could do whatever they wanted. We made the club song for that week 'Hi Ho Hi Ho, it's off to work we go' the Seven Dwarves' song, to accentuate this job of work.

My dad didn't make it that year. He died before we got to Wembley. I turned round in my seat to give my mother a kiss. She was reaching into her handbag for a miniature brandy and a glass she had fetched with her. I looked up to the row where my dad had sat so proud in his blazer the year before.

The son my father always wanted
Playing memories

☐ May 11th, 1967 I gave birth to the son my father had always wanted. The same day my mother was admitted to hospital; however, Rovers were to play at Wembley that Saturday so my father left her and went down to London. Rovers won the cup and my father could not have been happier had Littlewoods sent him a massive cheque. Imagine - the cup and a grandson!

In 1973 Rovers won the cup again and Cyril Kellet, who lived on the same estate as us, was my four year old's hero. We went up to Cressey's Corner to see the victory parade go by, and there on the open-topped bus was Simon's hero holding the cup aloft. We cheered and cheered. After we returned home, Simon went to his bedroom and in his enthusiasm for the day, leapt from the top bunk, breaking his arm in the fall. Another cup and another hospital visit for me.

☐ Scrum-halves are born either cocky or stupid, or so they say. I started at St. Helens when I was fourteen, signed on for them when I was sixteen and I was soon playing for the first team.

Vince wasn't the best player we had, but he'd have run through a wall if you'd asked him to. He took it on himself to work with me when I got into the team and set up a convoluted plan which involved patting me on the backside as part of the code. When he was ready to put it into action I completely ignored him and ran eighty yards to the touchline, then veered back to put the ball between the sticks.

☐ We had eleven stone, five foot eight Duggie Greenhaugh at St. Helens. He was a mean bugger though. When we beat Australia 44 - 8 he put six of them in hospital. Afterwards I said to him, 'Why Duggie?'

'I'm a pro, Spud. If I was marking my own mother, she'd have to go.'

When he went over to Aus, they'd heard about him. Twenty thousand turned out and some of them were laughing until he put another six in hospital.

☐ I was playing for Batley at York and it was pouring down with rain. I was going down for a loose ball when someone accidentally kicked me in the cheek after they had kicked the ball. Billy Smith, the coach, took a careful look and said he'd have to take out two of my teeth. We were stood at the side of the grandstand and two young girls were stood at the other side of the railings watching what was going on. Billy took out the teeth with his thumb and forefinger and held them up for all the crowd to see. I can still see the young lady fall over flat on her face in a pool of water.

☐ The most frightening time I had in Rugby League was at Widnes in 1976. Nobody and nothing will ever scare me after that, but that bleak afternoon in February will stay with me until my very last breath.

To this day I don't know the facts surrounding what happened, but at the time I didn't want to make a fuss. The whole episode must have lasted twenty-five seconds at most, but until you've writhed dying in front of a few thousand for that long, you really haven't lived!

All I can remember is being upended and landing awkwardly. Simultaneously a huge piece of my half-digested, fatty, landlady bacon breakfast came forward, at exactly the same time as a gill of gloppy mud hit the back of my throat.

Afterwards they said the confusion arose because I went down clutching my knee, which I maybe did. One of the weird things about choking to death is, the keener you are in drawing attention to your predicament, the vaguer you become with sign language. About three seconds from death I recall hearing derisive whistles from Leigh supporters, then my mate Keith walloped me between the shoulder blades with his instep.

I retched once and the blockage jamming my windpipe landed on the pitch. Fifteen seconds later I was up, and a more thoughtful player for a couple of minutes.

☐ When I first started playing I was only twelve stone. I used to get these big seventeen stone forwards coming up to me. They all had flat noses, broken teeth and cauliflower ears. They grunted and barked when they talked and they used to say thinks like, 'Look here young 'un, one thing tha's got to remember in this game, is to look after thissen.' When this comes from blokes who look like they've been whacked across the mush with a shovel you've got to laugh. Mind you, the medical attention wasn't up to much then. First time I got a bad knock the sponge man came running on, puffing and blowing with a cig in his mouth and said, 'Next time you go down Colin, do it nearer the bloody touchline, then I won't have to run so far.'

☐ The rough and tumble of Rugby League can seriously affect your looks. Jimmy Crossley was a horrible looking man but very distinctive. He was Castleford's big second row forward with ginger spiky hair, a broken nose and half his teeth were missing. I once took my father-in-law on holiday to Bridlington and one day he came into the caravan telling me of how he'd seen this horrific man drinking in the George Hotel and he gave me a very graphic description. I thought to myself, 'I bet I know who that is' and the next day I went down to the George Hotel with him. Sure enough, as I walked in the door there stood Jimmy. 'Now then Reg,' he called, 'are we having a drink?' and when he smiled three women fainted.

☐ My mate and me were sat on the seats on the touchline at Station Road and the game was getting very tense. Suddenly it exploded with both packs going at it hammer and tongs right in front of us. The next we knew, Warlow was laid out and his landlady was over the wall swinging her handbag at the Halifax forwards. The touch judge grabbed her, pushed her on to my mate's knee and said, 'Keep hold of her, mate, while we sort the players out.'

My mate said, 'I don't fancy this,' and pushed her on to me. I didn't fancy it either, she was a huge woman so I couldn't get my arms round her. Then two policemen came over, rescued me and firmly but politely escorted her up the tunnel. I've never been as glad to see a copper.

☐ Peter Jarvis played for Halifax. He was approaching the end of his career but wouldn't admit it to himself or anyone else. That was why he was becoming increasingly angry with the coach. The coach, an understanding, but of necessity, ruthless man, was in the habit of substituting Jarvis midway through the second half for some muscle bound youth with a crew cut. They always seemed to be called Jason or Craig. Peter and the coach had never really discussed the issue. Despite being near the end of his career, Jarvis still had a big contribution to make and he wanted to stay in a winning side, so neither wanted to rock the boat. Enough was enough. Peter had a plan. He would show the coach that he was still good value for the full eighty minutes.

Peter Jarvis played at open side prop. On the day of the next match, he removed the substitution board with the number eight on it from its satchel. Half way through the second half, when the time came, the coach would search in vain for the board with his number on it. He would stay on the field for the full eighty minutes and prove them all wrong.

Midway through the second half the moment of reckoning came. Jarvis looked expectantly towards the dugout from his position near a play the ball and saw, to his satisfaction, the coach rummaging frantically in

the substitution board satchel. He was just about to raise two fingers in his direction when, like a judge in an ice-skating contest, the coach raised the numbers seven and one above his head. Peter trudged from the field a beaten man.

☐ Keith Davies was a hard man, a fourteen-and-a-half stone sprinter who came from the Border sports to race at Powder Hall. He was second once to the world champion by a yard. When he tackled he crash-tackled and he sent the crowd berserk. I've never seen anybody put centres out like that. In one game he came up and said, 'Don't pass to me for a bit, my ankle's sore.' Then he started stamping and stamping but the pain wouldn't go away. He carried on stamping to shake it off and then at the end of the game we found out he'd played with a broken leg!

☐ Glenn Knight and Terry Day used to play for Cas' - so we had a Knight and Day. We also had Howard Bibb and a bloke called Tucker - Bibb and Tucker.

☐ Players have got a responsibility to their employers, the sponsors and to the fans. I don't want to see them uncomfortable in collars and ties wherever they go, but I don't expect them to be running around town drunk.

When I captained the lads at Wembley I wasn't nervous. The thing that got to me most of all was the thought of making the speech after the dinner when we got home. I sat on my own on the bus all the way back thinking about what I was going to say. When I saw my name on the menu it scared me to death.

Whether you're playing in a final at Wembley or in a league game at Salford you still go through the same pre-match ritual. Every player has his own ritual. I used to get up and have a bowl of Weetabix and that would be the last thing while after the game. I'd sit in the dressing room, perhaps read the programme for ten minutes and then start strapping up my fingers and thumbs, have a rub down and then do some exercises. That's when the butterflies start. Some players will go to the toilet three or four times. I always had a drop of Sal Volatile in water - that stops the flutters.

☐ Until I went to Barrow to play Rugby League the only time I had ever tasted fresh seafood was on working men's club trips to Bridlington. Two of my team mates, Mike Ducie and Bobby Little, taught me how to gather, prepare and cook all kinds of delicacies; cockles, mussels, lobster and crab. Another skill I never did get to master was 'fluke treading'. A fluke is a flat fish and the idea was to wade out at low tide and paddle gently, moving your feet along the sea bottom. If you were lucky you'd tread on a fluke and hold it there until you reached down for it. I suppose it's an unusual image of a Rugby League player, a man with his trousers rolled up, wading through the sea with a sawn down garden rake, hunting for cockles.

☐ When Paul Charlton came back from Salford he came to see me and said, 'Do you fancy doing some coaching, Phil?' We bought a couple of balls and put it in the *Whitehaven News* and *Barrow Evening Mail* that two ex-professionals were starting to coach kids. On the first night sixty turned up and we only had the two balls. The next day the pair of us went to the paper shop to buy a coaching book!

☐ During idle moments at the pit I often talked to the onsetter about his playing career and one day he mentioned that when he played and had a bad game he used to come off the field with several arrows in his back. 'What the hell do you mean?' I asked. 'Well' he said 'When I was playing, if you dropped the ball, missed a tackle, or made any sort of daft mistake, you'd look back towards the dugout and there would be the coach, firing arrers at you from an imaginary bow'. This amusing little tit-bit I tucked away at the back of my mind and had almost forgotten until years later when I'd left the pit and found another job.

Opposite to the place where I work there's the village pub and I often call for a quick one. The landlord happens to be an ex-Great Britain international forward. I usually go in when the pub is quiet, and talk always turns to Rugby. It wasn't long before I recalled the tale, related to me by his old buddy, about the latter day Sitting Bull, half expecting him to deny it. He laughed and affirmed that it was perfectly true. More than that, he told me the following story.

We were playing at St. Helens in a mid-week match and both sides were pressing for the title and so were thirsty for league points. It was a ding-donger of a game and the lead kept changing from one side to the other. Late in the game St. Helens went in front and we needed a try to grab the winning points. As the seconds ticked away we were pressing near their line and finally created a clear opening. The final pass went to a young second teamer who had just been promoted to the first team squad. He charged for the line. In desperation a St. Helens forward grabbed him as he went over and managed to turn him on his back. A pile of supporting defenders dropped on top. The referee signalled 'no try.' As the mound of bodies disentangled itself a lone prostrate figure lay over the line waiting to be carried off on a stretcher. The whistle blew and we had lost. Later, in the dressing room, an injured and battered teenager looked up at his coach for sympathy. All he got was, 'Don't think that it weren't St.Helens forwards that did thi. It were my arrers'.

Making a deep bow to the Threepenny Stand
Referees remember

☐ Laurie Thorpe was a little referee with a very sharp tongue. I was once playing at Hull for Batley in a really rough match and Laurie was having a hard time keeping control. Hull had scored and we were all stood behind the posts when somebody threw half a bottle of beer from the stand towards our now totally fed-up referee. He picked up the bottle and held it up to the crowd and shouted, 'Who threw that?' to which a burly docker replied, 'I bleeding did.' Laurie tossed it back to him and said 'Next time throw a full one.'

☐ The Threepenny Stand at Hull is always full of colour and humour and sometimes you've got to have a broad back, because the line there between humour and abuse is a thin one. In the early 1970s Hull F.C. decided to put their dugouts in front of the Threepenny Stand. They couldn't have done much worse. I went one Saturday as the committee rep for Leeds and had to sit and listen to some of the vilest epithets you can imagine. The taunt all Loiners have to put up with is the questioning of their Jewish ancestry. I've never heard anything like what they were coming out with that day at Hull. And then Peter Dunn, the Leeds hooker, got himself sent off. I had to walk him the full length of the touchline, all the way in front of wailing Airlie Birds. When we got to the dressing room I said, 'Peter, get your shower and don't come back out.' I knew what might happen if he did. Then it dawned on me. 'Bloody hell, I've got to walk all the way back in front of them!'

Nearly forty years before I had experienced the wrath of the Threepenny Stand. Oliver Morris, a great little stand-off half who only weighed nine and a half stone, was playing opposite the big bustling Hull man, Laurie Herbert. Oliver got more and more frustrated in his efforts, Herbert was a very strong man and Oliver never got past him all the game. Of course the Threepenny Stand were taunting Oliver, the more frustrated he became. In the end Oliver picked up two handfuls of mud and chucked it. It splattered everybody in the first four rows. Uproar! Oliver needed the protection of both teams and the bobbies and then only just got away safe.

☐ I've seen referee Holdsworth come over to the Threepenny Stand before a game, hold up his hands and bow to them. The Threepenny Stand are the most knowledgeable people in the game. They appreciate good Rugby. Even if their opponents score a try they will put their hands together. I don't think they ever forgave Garry Schofield though when he went from Hull to Leeds. He always played at right centre, but he played at left centre when he came back to Hull with Leeds so he wouldn't have to start the game off on the Threepenny Stand side. Once when Leeds came he had to take a goalkick on that side because Maskill had gone off. He got some abuse that day.

☐ To quote Woody Allen, 'It's not the despair, it's the hope that kills me.' I'm amazed how often this quote amply reflects a Rugby League match. Being robbed by referees is a regular event, as supporters from every team will tell you. It happens so often, it's part of the game. I can clearly recall one particularly diabolical incident in the Cup at Bradford. It was when players and officials had to walk through the crowd to get to the dressing rooms. On this particular occasion the referee had an escort of police, both on foot and mounted, lining his route, as disgruntled supporters hurled abuse and tried to set about him.

Another time, at Headingley, we were robbed of a well-deserved two points and during the course of the game, as a consequence of the ref's bad decisions, we got into an heated altercation with some Leeds fans. To add insult to the injury we felt by losing, we were reported by some Leeds lads to the Boys in Blue for racial harassment. Now that was an insult. Paul and Glynn, my mates, and myself are all staunch trade union activists and all vehemently anti-racist.

□ I was refereeing Swinton and Dewsbury and had just awarded a penalty. There was somebody injured, so I dropped my hanky and went over to where he was lying. As I did so there was a great roar of protest from the crowd. When I turned round there was nothing I could see.

Anyway, Albert Blan kicked the penalty and at half time I said to the touch judge, 'What were the crowd baying about?'

'I had to ask someone that myself,' he replied. 'Albert bloody Blan kicked the hanky ten yards closer to the sticks than you'd left it.'

□ Refs often come in for a lot of stick from Rugby League fans and in my opinion a lot of it is justified, although I do appreciate it is a difficult job. But even my dislike of refs is

nothing compared to the animosity felt toward them by an elderly Rovers fan who used to attend all first and second team games at home. If the truth be known, he probably only went to have a go at the ref. All decisions, good or bad, which went against his team, were met with his favourite cry of, 'Get thi bleedin' eyes tested.' On one occasion, the man in the middle had a particularly lousy game and came under heavy verbal fire from the now octogenarian ref-baiter, who extended his vocabulary to include 'Bloody rubbish ref, where's thi white stick?' and 'Tha wants to swallow that bleedin' whistle.'

A fortnight later at the next second team home game the ref was the same as on the previous occasion. This time, however, he played a blinder and never put a foot wrong. As he was coming down the tunnel at the end of the match, our hero came up to the fence and sneered, 'By, tha were rubbish Ref, but tha wern't as bad as him we had last week.'

□ Councillor Arnold Bagnall is due to become Rochdale's Mayor next year. A life long Hornets fan, in his younger days (the 50s and 60s) he was a regular touch judge. Arnold's claim to fame was that he was probably the fastest touch judge in Rugby League. His party piece came after he had stood behind the posts to signal a goal. As soon as his flag was down he would

zoom back to the halfway line and arrive there way before anyone else.

Picture Wigan in a cup tie. Arnold is one of the touch judges and Wigan have the ball on their own line. Suddenly the ball is swung out to Billy Boston, Wigan's flying winger, who hurtles down the touchline for more than 90 yards, outstripping all the opposition. Who's waiting for him over the try line and saying, 'Put it down there, Billy?'

□ I refereed a match between Greenacres and Higginshaw in 1948. My cousin, Jack Read was the captain of Greenacres. His father of the same name played for Oldham Rugby League Football Club and was one of the team when Oldham last won the Cup in 1927. Cousin Jack was continually disagreeing with my decisions against his side in the first half so, after two or three remarks, I called him to me. 'You! Come here. What's your name?' I asked. 'I'm your bloody cousin,' he replied angrily. I said quite calmly, 'I'll only ask you once more, and if you don't answer correctly you are in the dressing room!' to which he replied, 'Jack Read.' 'Right,' I said, 'I know you're the captain, but from now on keep your mouth shut or else you're off.'

When he went home, his mother, my Aunt Ivy, was confronted by an angry son. Jack flung

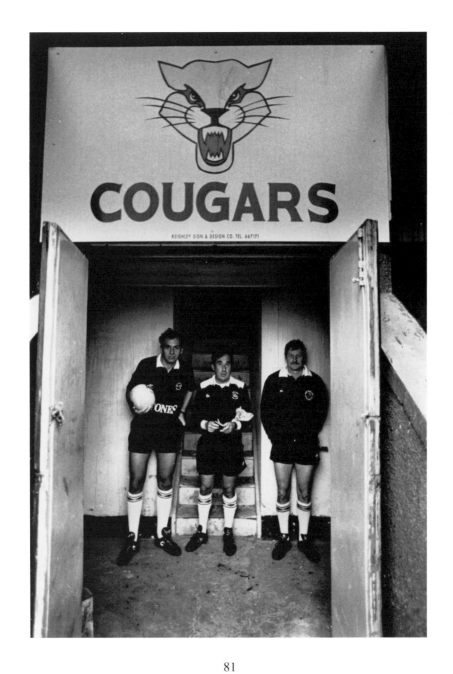

his kit in the kitchen and turned to his mother. 'Mother, what do you think?' he said angrily. 'Our Dick asked me for my name today and cautioned me.' Her reply was, 'Yes, our Dick would.'

☐ Leeds were playing Swinton in a John Player Trophy Third Round Cup Tie in November 1983. Swinton did not have a strong side at all in those days and to Leeds followers at the Cup Tie it appeared the result would be a foregone conclusion, it was merely a question of how many points Leeds would run up. After all, a star-studded line-up included such players as Dean Bell from New Zealand, Terry Webb and Mark Laurie from Australia, plus several Great Britain internationals, including David Ward, Kevin Dick and David Creasser.

It all started to go wrong for Leeds from the first minute as the home-spun Swinton side, playing with admirable spirit, overwhelmed their illustrious visitors and quickly built up a ten point lead which they still held at half-time.

Leeds had been a lack-lustre side for the first forty minutes. During the break an excellent and enthusiastic Lancashire brass band entertained the fans and were given such a warm reception that they became reluctant to leave the field to allow the game to restart. Referee Ronnie Campbell became quite agitated and began to demand the band clear the field. The cheeky Leeds scrum half, Kevin Dick, walked across to Ron and said, 'Let them stay on, Ronnie. We'll go back to the dressing rooms, after all they're playing a lot better than we are!'

Leeds showed better form in the second half and eventually scraped home by 16 points to 12. In fact they went on to finally win the trophy.

☐ Sunday morning amateur Rugby League must have been invented by men who didn't go for a drink on Saturday nights. Nowadays it is often played by lads who still have their beer in them. This can lead to many an amusing incident. I once tackled a little fat player who then started to bite my hand.

'Ref! Ref! He's biting me!' I shouted.

'Well, take your bloody hand out of his mouth!' came the reply.

In a later game this ref disallowed us a winning try with the scores locked at 4 - 4. Following the decision, our opponents moved the ball quickly upfield and dropped what looked like the winning goal when the ref's whistle sounded. We thought we had lost, but then he told us the whistle was blown before the ball crossed between the sticks. As our opponents rounded on him, he stood his ground and uttered the words, 'A draw was a fair result!'

☐ At a recent amateur game I heard cries of 'Forward pass, are you blind ref?' Hearing this the ref turned round to see a lone spectator, ageing, bespectacled, fifty yards behind the play and in fading light.

☐ A crowd will soon sense that you've got no bottle. If you want to be a referee, you've got to have courage. When I became the Controller of Referees I always watched the young referees do the assault course when we held seminars. Two things I examined them for were fitness and courage.

I started refereeing after I lost a kidney as a teenage player. I learned very early on that the third attribute you need after fitness and courage is preparation. I was in charge of a match at Askern, got changed into my kit in the miners' bath house and then realised Id forgotten to pack my whistle. I quietly asked the lamp man if he had one, hoping he'd keep it to himself. Instead he shouted down the room, 'Eh! oop! Ref's no whistle!' I felt a complete fool, and even more stupid when I had to walk in my refereeing gear to the local shop to see if they sold them. I eventually got one from the fire station. That has always stuck in my gullet. I've never been unprepared since that time.

My normal Sunday morning routine would be to get up, walk down for the Sunday papers,

have some tea and toast and then go for a walk and a stretch. Then I would come back and clean my kit, thinking all the time about that afternoon's game. My missus would leave me alone apart from routine conversations while I would build myself up for the match, totally psyching myself until I was almost in a trance. When I arrived at the ground I would try to have a sleep in the car for an hour. Experience over the years taught me that if you go into the ground too early all you get is the groundsman or somebody coming up and complaining about the previous week's referee.

☐ Have you noticed that when you attend a match in which you have no partisan interest, the standard of refereeing improves considerably?

☐ Leigh were playing Liverpool Stanley at Leigh. Having no car in those early days, I went via local bus to Salford bus station and caught the bus to Leigh. The bus was just pulling out when a ginger haired young fellow jumped on. It was Jimmy Winterbottom who played hooker for Liverpool Stanley. We sat together because we knew each other very well. I worked for Oldham Parks Department and Jim worked for the Gas and Water Department. After we had been travelling about half an hour I just glanced at my watch and to my dismay it had stopped, but Jimmy straight away offered to loan me his and I accepted with thanks.

Now midway through the first half I had occasion to penalise Jim for 'Feet Up' in the scrum. I called him to me and said, 'Look Jimmy, you know what I'm like for good scrums. Feet back until the ball hits the deck in the centre of the tunnel. Next time you're off!' Leigh took the penalty kick into touch which was the procedure in those days, then a scrum was formed on the ten yard mark opposite where the ball crossed the touchline.

The Leigh scrum half threw the ball in the tunnel and lo and behold Winterbottom had his foot up again. I called out Winterbottom at the same time pointing for a penalty to Leigh. 'Dressing room!' and as he walked past me he said, 'Bloody hell, Dickie. I didn't think you would send me off after I had loaned you my watch.' I promptly replied, 'That was your first mistake.'

Even these days if ever he meets me in Oldham, even if he is across the street, he will point to his watch and call out, 'What time is it you bastard'.

☐ Of course referees notice the crowd reactions. There isn't a job that wouldn't be affected by somebody leaning over and booing. And sometimes it gets to us and we get pissed off. When I reffed the 1978 Challenge Cup semi-final between Widnes and St. Helens I knew before the start I was in for a hard time. There was a crowd of fifteen thousand in by 2 o'clock smelling for spilt blood. Alex Murphy had put it in the papers during the week that if Widnes won he would jump off Runcorn Bridge. Then when the game started Laughton and Nicholls were having a go at each other every tackle. I worked hard to keep them on, but in the end I couldn't stand them any more, so off they went. The Widnes full back then galloped the length of the field to smack Hesford for no reason and so off he went as well.

The half-time hooter blew while all this was going on. People ran on to the field, directors, police, tea ladies, dogs - it was just like going to a hanging. I sat in the dressing room at half-time and thought, 'I've got another forty minutes of this to come.' Things got worse and I ended up sending another three off. The dressing rooms were buzzing at the end of the game. Radio Merseyside, Radio Manchester, the Chief of Police all asking, 'Are you alright, Fred?' I said, 'No, I've had a bad day. They've insulted me, I'm pissed off and I'm going straight home.' In the end my two touch judges got me to go in to the board room for a cup of tea.

Another time I was at Keighley reffing them and Whitehaven. It was just after the sin-

bin had been introduced. The rule was that if a man was sin-binned he had to go to cool off in a room. I checked to see if Keighley had a room before the match started and they hadn't so I agreed with the trainers that if I sinbinned anybody they could sit on the bench. Sure enough, two players started fighting, so I sin binned the Whitehaven man. Then half way through the first-half Keighley scored a try and while I was waiting for the conversion I heard the crowd laughing. I turned round and there's a bloody bloke stood behind me. I said, 'Who the bloody hell are you?' He said, 'I'm a Keighley director and I've got a complaint.'

'What are you talking about?'

'You've let that Whitehaven man affect play by sitting on the bench.'

So I said, 'If you got a bloody room sorted out, he wouldn't be on the bench.'

Half an hour later the touch judge put his flag up and I went over to see what was the matter. He said, 'This bloke's just punched me.'

I was getting fed up with all this, so I said, 'Right, where is he?' He pointed him out in the crowd. I stopped the game and said I wouldn't start it again until the police had thrown him out. The crowd started booing and carrying on but I wasn't having my touch judges punched.

You can prepare as much as you like for a game, but you can't budget for what might happen. I always used to tell the young refs that. Let the game unfold, then referee accordingly, never try to prejudge.

To add insult to injury that day at Keighley I nearly laid myself out. They have an RSJ supporting the roof as you go into the dressing room. I looked round and banged my head on the beam as I went in.

☐ Dobson was a very strict referee. He was in charge of a right rough encounter at Hull. I was playing for Batley and we were beating them, the crowd were going mad, the dockers had been screaming at Dobson from the terraces throughout the whole game. Hull scored in the dying minutes but had to score again to win. As we got back to the half-way line Dobson said to our Aussie scrum-half Hector Gee, 'I'll be glad when this bloody game is over. As soon as the ball goes into touch I'll be off down that tunnel.' Freddie Miller lined up the kick-off and was intent on booting it out of the ground but he fluffed it, and Hull gathered the ball and drove it down to our line, leaving the ref sixty yards to run back to the tunnel. Dobson covered that distance faster than Brian Bevan.

☐ Leigh used to have as their right winger in the late 50s and early 60s a player called Ernie Hudson, not a great player but a loyal club servant. Unfortunately he was very short sighted and when he wasn't playing he used to wear very thick glasses. He didn't carry a white stick, but he did have a Labrador! This was in the days before players used contact lenses.

I was once at a particular match when Leigh came out with a magnificent passing movement, the ball moved swiftly along the line and ended up in the arms of Ernie Hudson on the right wing. He sidestepped his marker and beat the full-back for speed, diving over to score in the corner. He turned around to meet the applause of the crowd and the handshakes of his team mates, but was greeted with stony faces and hushed silence. To his horror he had scored one of the best tries of the season, but on the 25 yard line instead of the goal line!

☐ About 1961, Rochdale Hornets brought six Fijians over. The first to arrive was Laitia Ravouvou (Lijah to his friends). He was a massive man who took size 14 boots. His first game was at Leigh. Jim Parr took him to one side in the dressing room and said, 'You'll be alright Lijah. Just sort their prop out. Hit him hard early on and he won't want to know. He's a big soft sod. You can't miss him, the one with the bald head.'

It was only Stan Owen, one of the hardest men around at that time! So they take to the field and Hornets kick-off with a high floating ball which Stan rises for and gathers, but he also gets Lijah who had come thundering through, totally upending him. Hard as he was, Stan was left shaken on the ground. A couple of grunts and a shake of the head and Stan was up to see Jim Parr grinning like a Cheshire cat and nodding to Lijah. As soon as they noticed him staring, they knew Stan had it sussed.

Jim Parr is on record as saying he knew poor Lijah would cop for it then.When the next scrum broke up, things began to happen. In Jim's words, 'A sledgehammer caught me in the eye and as they carried me off, I saw Stan smile at me and nod to Lijah.' That was the first of many tussles between Stan and Lijah before they became team mates at Rochdale.

One thing about Stan Owen when he was at Leigh, the cry from Hornets fans, me included, was, 'Get the dirty bastard off!' but when he donned the red, white and blue we changed our tune; now it was, 'Go on Stan get 'em cracked!'

☐ Just before half time Laurie Thorpe, a proper Wakefield gentleman, blew the whistle and dropped to the ground. We could see he was dead as they carried him past the stand. Just before they left the ground they covered his face. The touch judge refereed the second half.

Great men don't come any greater
Rugby Legends

☐ A few months ago I was successful in acquiring a new post at a nursing home situated on the outskirts of Leeds. This nursing home specialises in the care and treatment of those suffering from Alzheimers disease. Briefly, this ailment affects the ability to remember and the faculty to co-ordinate thoughts. The first duty I was given was to see to the needs of a particular resident. I walked into the room and recognised the face immediately: it was Cyril Kellett.

All through that day I reflected on some of the games that I could remember him playing and some of his achievements. One game, an insignificant one in Rugby history, stuck in my mind as it illustrated the value of a man who, through the use of his talents, could keep his team in the game and eventually turn near-certain defeat into triumph. I was sure that among my old scrap books I somewhere had a cutting about that match. I hurried home at the end of my duties and rummaged through the tattered pages. To my relief I found what I was looking for.

The game was a league match that took place on 28th August 1965 at Parkside, Hunslet. Cyril then played for Hull K.R. and on this day put in a vintage performance. Cyril's trusty boot had given his side an early lead but Hunslet were in a determined mood and soon took control of the game and by half-time had a handsome lead. A change of ends can often bring a change of fortunes and as this new half began, Hunslet started to make some silly mistakes which was suicide when Cyril was around. A few penalties within his range were safely converted, a carefully worked move had Cyril over the line and before you knew it, Hull K.R. were in front 19 - 17, all their points scored by one man. With their nose's in front, the men from Humberside began to take charge and strolled out to a comfortable win. Kellett finished with a personal tally of eleven goals and one try. It was a superb display of one man plugging away, inching his team back into contention and then on to final victory.

Sadly, Cyril died in March 1993. He will be missed by anybody who knows about Rugby League on whichever ground they watch it.

☐ Great men don't come any greater than Neil Fox, a veritable points-scoring machine who probably received every honour going in Rugby League. Never sent off during his very long career, never that is, until he clashed with Peter Clarke, the Hornets' Number nine. Thereby hangs a tale.

It was 1976 and Hornets had to travel to York for the last game of the season - if Hornets won, they got promotion; if they lost, Hull got it.

When we got to York we thought we were on the wrong ground. Hull had shipped a large support over to cheer York on. Within about fifteen minutes we were trailing 12 - 2 and things were looking grim. All York's moves were coming off Neil Fox who, although at the end of his career, still had a great rugby brain and was very strong. As the game went on, Clarky niggled Foxy a few times but nothing happened. Then Clarky finally got to him. A bust up ended with Clarky flat out and the ref pointing to the dressing room for Fox. When Clarky got up, he got the same message. The outcome was York were like a ship without a rudder and Hornets took control winning twenty odd points to eighteen. I must say Alan Hodgkinson and Dave Hawley were magnificent that day. Clarky still gets ribbed for fox hunting out of season.

☐ Terry Clawson has to be one of the greatest of Rugby League characters, he was forever having the crack. The way he drops the one-liners, he's a dry bugger. I call them *Clawsonisms*. Roger Millward told me about the time Hull K.R. played St. Helens in the third round. At that time Roger had never been to Wembley, but with not long to go the Robins were winning 10 - 8. Then the Saints player, Wilson, picked up a loose ball, beat about five men and went the length of the field to score. This put the Robins out of the cup. As they walked back to kick off, Roger was nearly roaring. He knew his chance had gone again. He looked round at Clawson, his team mate, who said almost in a whisper, 'What a wonderful try!'

On the 1974 Tour Clawson was already a veteran and he was up against the mighty Art Beetson, then in his pomp. The press in Oz were really bumming up their hero. In the first game there was an horrendous collision between Clawson and Beetson, but old Terry was the first up. He smiled at the grounded Beetson, smiled at the other Aussie players, pointed at a huge figure in green and gold and said, 'Who's she?'

☐ Eddie Waring was quite extraordinary. I found him to be a gentleman and an absolute professional. 'Early bath' and 'Up and under' became catchwords down here in Hampshire because of him. I first met him in Southampton when he was doing *Jeux sans Frontieres* and a while later he took me to my first game in Leeds with the words, 'Come and see a real football game.' I was converted immediately. I'd never seen anything like it.

☐ I first met Jim Gath when I visited Wilton Park, Batley, as a boy aged about nine. He scared me as I was up an oak tree at the time collecting acorns! He was the park ranger, a fearsome chap. He shouted at me and waved his stick. I jumped down and sprinted off.

On a hot day later on he found me having a nose bleed so he put a large iron key down the back of my neck and the bleeding stopped through shock!

When I grew up I visited Jim occasionally to take him fruit and chat about Rugby League. He was a member of the Batley team in 1897 which won the first ever Challenge Cup Final, defeating St. Helens by ten points to three.

When Jim remarried when a pensioner, we were photographed together outside the Registry Office. Jim confided in me with a chuckle that illegal payments to Rugby Union players were not new as, when he played Rugby Union in the 1890s, he received small financial rewards after games walking around to a local industrialist's home to collect his money.

☐ Of course there's the memories but the rest is a collection of various bits of paper in a sideboard drawer. There's the authorisation papers of the Provisional Government of Latvia which allows his father August Rixman of Sophia Street, Tiger Bay, Cardiff, to travel with

his son, aged nine, back across war-torn Europe. Then there is the picture of a schoolboy player with medals pinned to his jersey. Like many sons of immigrants, he is moving into an area where he can succeed without too much prejudice; into sports or entertainment.

A typed note records that he signed for Salford in 1929 for £25 down and £1 per week for a year. A scroll photograph of the English Rugby League touring side of 1932 with the remarkable Welshman eighth from the left hand side is there along with other photos. Gus Risman's marriage, Gus as military policeman and in rugby gear. The medals and the trophies are elsewhere, shared out among his children and grandchildren.

Someone has written down the statistics of twenty seven remarkable seasons: Salford, Dewsbury and Leeds, Workington Town, then, in the last season, Batley. When he was 45 years old he scored 294 points. What a record!

Of course there is a big picture on the wall at Rugby League Headquarters, but these are the also-rans, yet more significant for all that: what looks to be a press photograph of him in his sports outfitters with half-opened boxes behind him, passports which show him growing middle-aged and then old. A Prince Charles and Lady Di photography album contains family photographs including some of his sons in an international match, for this is a rugby dynasty. An old man at a Christmas party has emerged from the rugby warrior who conquered all there was to conquer.

☐ Rugby League is a very physical sport and can lead to serious injuries and sometimes death. I can remember a brilliant young player called John Burke who was born in Leigh but made his name elsewhere, at Workington. He was a Great Britain Colt, and looked to have a dazzling future. However, one bad tackle was enough to banish him to a wheelchair for the rest of his life with horrific spinal injuries.

☐ The worst injury I had playing was from a knee in the eye. I wouldn't mind but I saw it coming, only I couldn't get out of the way. It knocked my eyeball back in the socket.

I was playing for Oldham at the time so I ended up in Withington Hospital. The doctors told me I would be out for a long time. So I picked up the budgie, the dog and the wife and went back home to Cumbria.

☐ When I played for West Hull at full back I got knocked out in three successive games. They were going to pick me for the fourth game, so I turned round and said, 'Nay, even a bloody boxer gets a rest!'

I got my rest a bit later up in Egremont, Cumberland. One of their forwards stiff-armed me and I got an 'L' shaped break in my top two neck vertebrae. I ended up in hospital in Whitehaven for a long time.

☐ Getting injured is a common thing in most contact sports and Rugby League is no exception. It's accepted by the players but there's being hurt and there's being injured. Most injuries clear up in two weeks, some take a little longer, some like mine will never heal in a lifetime. I have seen ex-players slowly deteriorate until they either don't know who they are or can't walk around. For me, my life of walking around ended abruptly one cold Sunday morning on a muddy miners' welfare field in Brodsworth, Doncaster. I was playing hooker for a local amateur Rugby League club. Everything was okay until half way through the first half. Just as the Saturday night's beer had drained from my head we went down for a scrum and I received a bang to the top of my skull. I must say I believed and still do that it was an accident and blame no-one. I fell to the ground in no pain, but I had no movement either. As usual the ambulance seemed to take ages but really it took only 5 to 10 minutes and I was on my way to Doncaster Royal Infirmary where X-rays showed a dislocation of my neck - a high

dislocation, and the vertebrae had also been crushed and would have to be operated on straight away.

The next thing I knew was a thumping great headache and feeling the worst I've ever felt. My neck had been operated on and only time would tell the extent of the damage. It did. After a few weeks lying on my back I knew I would never walk again and soon a new kind of life would begin for me.

My father once told me amateur Rugby is for has-beens and never-will-be's. That was twenty years ago. Now I believe it's true, but I continue my alliance with the miners' welfare as the club secretary. Team spirit seemed to go down after my injury and the club kept getting relegated. Now we are on the up, my ambition is to help them get back to the top.

☐ When I was a younger player and I used to hurt them, they would get up saying, 'You big, ugly bastard.' Now I'm at the veteran stage and I still hurt them. They get up saying, 'You big, bald-headed bastard.'

☐ Vince Farrar and Sammy Windmill were young bloods making their way in the game, gaining experience which would stand them in good stead in the first team by putting in some hair raising performances in the reserves. Vince

in particular was a cult figure. He was a member of the crew of Thunderbird One, the Featherstone Urban District Council dustbin waggon. Two of his shipmates were Leslie Tonks and Arnold Morgan, famous first teamers who had played at Wembley for the Rovers, so the people of the village could rest easy knowing that their rubbish was in such safe hands.

Denis Morgan provided the 'old head' in the Rovers Reserve grade front row at the time. He had never made the big time, but had a reputation for being, shall we say, 'uncompromising'. The front-row formation would usually be Farrar as hooker, with Windmill and Morgan as his prop forwards.

In the days before the Rovers had floodlights, games would be played at the end of the season in the early evening sunshine. It was a good feeling going to these games. The worst of the winter was over, the light nights were back, hence the evening kick-off. There was always an air of festival in the crowd at these games which were usually held on a Monday.

So it was on this particular evening when Rovers Reserves were playing their Castleford counterparts in the semi-final of the Yorkshire Senior Competition Shield. The good weather, the local rivalry, the fact that the game was one step away from a trophy, plus the presence of our three heroes in the side meant that there was

a crowd of about five thousand and an atmosphere full of portent.

They were not to be disappointed. The catalyst which was to set in motion the chain of events was Tony Miller, the Castleford hooker. Like Farrar and Windmill, he was young and wanting to catch the eye. He'd also locked horns with the pair several times during the winter.

Straight from the kick-off there was an air of barely restrained violence on the field. You got the feeling that the players were just waiting for an excuse. Predictably this came with the first scrum. Farrar's head jerked up from the huddled mass of bodies and violently back as if in some kind of spasm. The scrum disintegrated leaving Farrar on his knees, shaking his head and wiping the blood from his mouth.

Ten minutes later another scrum, only this time it was Denis's turn to stagger away like a marionette with its string cut. The Rovers' pack were showing commendable and uncharacteristic restraint, but something was bound to give. The crowd were either loving it, seeing the Rovers supposed hard men smacked about, or confused who in the Castleford pack was causing this mayhem?

Just before half-time there was another scrum, the last one of the half. You could have heard the smack in Purston Park. Sure enough it was Sam Windmill who was being brought round by the Rovers' physio whose equipment for on-field injuries in those days was an enamel bucket filled with water and a dubious-looking sponge.

Sammy had come round enough to meander uncertainly from the field when the half-time whistle went. The crowd, during the half-time discussion, seemed to come to a general consensus that, although they didn't know who was dishing out the clockwinders with apparent impunity, Sammy, Vince and Denis did and wouldn't take it lying down, so to speak. Expectations were running high, the crowd sensed sparks would fly, but nobody could have predicted what actually happened.

The two teams trotted on to the field, the Rovers' front row looking particularly preoccupied. There were a few minor scuffles during the first twenty minutes or so of the second half and some great football. A scrum formed on the half-way line and the mayhem began. Fists, elbows, heads and knees rhythmically yet frenziedly pounding and grabbing. This was exactly what the crowd had expected, but then a terror-stricken figure detached itself from the savage melee. It was Tony Miller. Tony ran for the bogus sanctuary of the touchline as if a pack of rabid dogs were after him, but it was worse than that - Vince Farrar, Sammy Windmill and Denis Morgan had

decided that enough was enough. They made for Miller with vengeance in their hearts.

Surprisingly the crowd didn't bay for Tony Miller's blood, the Rovers contingent that is. Instead, probably uniquely, there was a unity in the crowd. A unity of dumbfoundedness as with the swiftness of thought of a cornered fox he leapt over the fence and ran up the terracing through the crowd, which parted, then closed as he passed through them. This unintentionally denied Vince, Denis and Sammy access to their prey who showed pace and vision far beyond anything he had ever displayed on the field of play.

He ran down the ash which was at the back of the terracing at the side of the stand, through the big main gates which were always thrown open at half time, up Post Office Road and into Station Lane. From the bottom of the Lane trundled the New Sharlston-Castleford circular bus. Miller leapt on board as it drew level with Schofield's tripe shop. What did the conductress say when she was confronted by a bruised and bleeding Rugby League hooker in his amber and black strip, with fear in his eyes? They didn't always give you an excess fare ticket if they didn't like the look of you. We shall never know but that rather dishevelled double decker was Tony Miller's 'little ship' at his own personal Dunkirk.

Steeped in the Game
Where we watch Rugby League

☐ I had to miss the 1973 Final because I had our Jane, the eldest, just a few days before; nature doesn't wait for Rugby League. But I dressed her up in blue and white and took her to watch them come home. I can remember standing at the top of Andrew Street with the pram, waving to the open-top bus.

When we were kids our mams and dads took us to games almost out of a sense of duty. Now they don't have that responsibility because there are Junior Supporters' Clubs which cater for young fans. There's also a much wider cross-section of people coming to matches now, both geographically and socially. You get to know supporters from as far apart as Rotherham and Ripon and I've seen women coming in high heels and their best coats. It's different. You've only to go back a generation and you'd find that players, spectators and administrators might live in the same street.

☐ Simon was in his Moses basket when we made him a member at Whitehaven. He was one day old and his number was 007. Straight away he won the club draw and two tickets for the next game, but we didn't actually take him to his first game until he was three.

☐ I have sold raffle tickets, lottery tickets, walked twenty miles twice from Sheffield to Featherstone dressed in the team colours (including my hair) to raise £600 each time, but the greatest sacrifice I made was a sponsored silence for the whole of the Eagles - Warrington game. I was only allowed to speak during half-time. The other eighty minutes seemed like an eternity. Rugby League is an audience participation sport and how the referee controlled that game without me telling him which passes were 'forrard', who had 'knocked on' and who was off-side, I'll never know.

☐ The BARLA Yorkshire Cup Final played at Belle Vue had all the prospects of being a cracking game of Rugby League. Two top local amateur teams pitched against each other. It was the first time that two Wakefield-based sides had contested the final and both Westgate Redoubt and Normanton were not going to give up the chance of the silverware lightly.

That this game was played at Belle Vue at all owes a lot to some shrewd manoeuvring in certain smoke-filled rooms. The RFL vs BARLA shenanigans meant that, technically, amateur teams were banned from playing at professional grounds. This was overcome since Wakefield MDC still own Belle Vue so the game was on. But hold on, the floodlights

belong to Wakefield Trinity so they can't be used and then there was a bit of argy-bargy about the dressing rooms but eventually the game was on and those who were there to witness it will never forget what they saw.

The Rugby itself was played, as you might expect, with all the intensity of a local derby but it will not be the Rugby that this game will be remembered for. With Normanton leading 8 - 6 at half-time we were all expecting an eventful second half but none of us were prepared for the drama that was about to unfold. The second half was a mass of stoppages for various incidents both on and off the field. First came a coin throwing incident which brought all three match officials over to the dugouts and a warning that if the incident was repeated the officials might abandon the match. As the game proceeded it was punctuated with stoppages for injuries and waiting for somebody to fetch the ball every time it was kicked out of the ground! It was during one of these stoppages that the most bizarre incident I have ever seen at a Rugby League game took place. Two men emerged from the crowd at the club-house end wearing nothing but shoes, socks and a smile, and started to run across the pitch with stewards in hot pursuit. The first man successfully negotiated the wall at the other side of the ground and disappeared up the terracing. The second man

went sprawling full length on the concrete terracing. A deafening 'Oooooh' went round the ground and the stretcher team who were on their way to an injured player were stuck in the middle trying to decide who to attend to first, player or streaker!

The game eventually restarted with a ball taken from a small boy who was playing on the terracing with his friends and, as darkness descended all around, Westgate just sneaked a victory.

☐ I had captained a number and variety of soccer teams and had been spotted by Wolverhampton Wanderers, so when I came up north I expected to do as I had always done, that is find a team that would have me and settle in quickly. It wasn't like that. The area I came to was dominated by Rugby League.

Rugby up to that time was a game played by people who lived in a different strata of society from me - their homes in leafy suburbs not at the back of lock-up shops or in council houses. They had been to grammar schools, not to the tech. They went to Oxford and came out with Blues, they didn't do City and Guilds and aspire to Higher Nationals. As a youth I read about them in the *Hotspur* or *Wizard*. When they went to away games rugby players wore blazers and cravats. They were called Toby and if they

married, it would be in little country churches, the fifteen lining the gravel walkway, to young women called Prudence but nicknamed Prue. They were superior beings. I had four mates called Brian going out with four girls called Pat when I left the Midlands. Rugby players chose more exclusive names. I didn't realise that there were two games called Rugby. Why should I? There was no television coverage of League; Twickenham was Rugby, not Post Office Road. I did not see that one was close to me and one as distant as the dreaming spires and quiet cloisters of cathedral towns.

☐ My wife Jean claims that Rugby is my religion - well, I was christened by a Rugby League referee. He was the Reverend Frank Chambers, a former player with Huddersfield who subsequently went on to become one of the leading referees of his era. He refereed the 1924 Cup Final between Wigan and Oldham.

If the Reverend Frank had pointed me in the right direction I got off to a good start when I first started to walk. I stumbled from my father to Len Bowkett, also a player with Huddersfield. Len was a former Coventry Rugby Union player and my father was proud of the fact that he had introduced him to League and was responsible for him signing for Huddersfield. Len played for Huddersfield for ten years and was their captain

at Wembley in 1933 when they beat Warrington by 21 - 17. His contribution was six goals from six attempts.

It would seem that Jean is right about my religion. She is wrong, though, when she claims that if it came to a choice between her and Rugby she doesn't fancy her chances - it would depend who was playing!

☐ I'm steeped in the game. Coming from Wigan it was inevitable. First being in the Hen Pen at Central Park and being close enough to touch the players as they came out of the tunnel, then following the team on a charabanc before the M6 or M62 to far away places with strange sounding names like Workington, Dewsbury and Hunslet. I was there on 25th February 1960, when Wigan beat Wakefield Trinity in the 2nd round of the Cup at Belle Vue behind the sticks where Fred Griffiths kicked the only score of the match. Drenched to the skin I can still taste the boiled ham and mustard butty that the coach driver gave me in pity when I got on the coach. The wet and cold didn't matter: we'd won. I was still there when Wigan lost to Whitehaven at the Recreation Ground on a cold wet Wednesday evening on 31st March 1982, amongst a crowd of a few hundred in the era before the present golden age and record crowds, thinking what the hell am I doing here.

☐ I would have been about eleven or twelve years old, just into long trousers, when I first went to see Castleford play in an away match. They had been drawn against the mighty Bradford Northern at Odsal and it was a match I dearly wanted to see.

At first I'd had a flat refusal from my mam when I'd asked her for money for the trip but, after much sulking, whining and pleading, she'd agreed to pay my train fare. That left me with the problem of how to find the money for the entrance fee. It can't have been much but when you're flat broke even a few pence seems like a lot of cash.

Eventually I had a flash of inspiration. My only viable asset was in a shoe box under my bed. In this box, nestled on a bed of flour, was my collection of wild birds' eggs. These were the culmination of a couple of years climbing trees, foraging in hedgerows and splodging about in muddy marshes. They were my pride and joy, but I was desperate for the cash, and I knew I had a buyer.

Tubby Watts, who lived down our street, was an only child and he wasn't allowed to go bird nesting and come home scratched, wet and filthy. This was my ticket; he'd buy them. The upshot was that I went off to see Tubby and duly sold him my prized possession for the princely sum of 1/6d.

Looking back all these years to the match, I don't remember much of the actual play. What I do recall is that when the train left Cas station, great gobs of snow had begun to fall. When we arrived at the ground, it was more like the Arctic than Odsal bowl. Vivid in my memory is the sight of men with sweeping brushes keeping the touchlines clear.

Rugby League records will show that Cas were narrowly beaten that day and Northern duly went on to the Final. There was one young lad stood on the terraces, his feet like blocks of ice in his thin black wellies and a wet woollen balaclava slowly freezing to his head who would never forget that day. I had seen my first away match. I had seen the Great Britain captain, Ernest Ward. Was it worth it? It was worth every egg!

☐ A cousin of mine was at a luncheon in Brisbane. When he said he was from Hunslet one of the Aussies said, 'Hunslet is the vilest place on earth; black houses, rain and blast furnaces belching flames up into the sky; it's like hell.' My cousin knew why he was saying that. In 1929 Hunslet beat Australia 18 - 3 and they say Hunslet only let Australia score so they could get back to the halfway line. I was brought up at Mother Bensons end at Parkside. There was a bloke there with waterproof trousers on, whose sole job was to fish the ball out of the beck every time it got kicked in. I never thought I'd end up the bloody President.

☐ My first game in Lancashire was as a seventeen year old with Wakefield at Salford. As we were walking onto the pitch I said to my team mate Harry Murphy, 'There's not much grass is there?' to which the Salford loose forward, Featham, replied 'You haven't come to bleeding graze.'

☐ The new Blackpool ground was built on the old gasworks site. Such was the rush to get it finished in August that as schoolboys we helped to barrow cinders around to get the terraces finished. Salford were the first visitors on a hot summer's afternoon. Borough won 36 -16 in a superb open game. It felt more like a garden party - beautiful manicured green grass and big white hospitality marquees, just for the opening game.

☐ One of the greatest amateur grounds has to be Back o't'Wall at Sharlston near Herbert Goodfellow's pub. The Sharlston lads once beat the mighty Workington Town team there. All the players used to pay tuppence apiece to a pensioner for lighting the coal boiler for the bath water. It bought him a few pints.

☐ At the old Hunslet club they had a traditional cricket ground next to the rugby field. The French were on tour over here and had brought a number of supporters with them. The groundsman for the cricket section came in and said, 'There are Frenchmen all over the cricket field.'

Somebody said, 'Leave them be, they're not doing any harm.'

The groundsman came back with, 'I believe they are fornicating on my best wicket.'

☐ In 1922 Hull Kingston Rovers left Craven Street to go to Craven Park. In my memories of seeing some good games there is the Rovers versus Wakefield match. Shortly before half-time there was one of those great Rugby League moments. Wakefield's Harry Street got the ball, just in his own half, on the right-hand side of the field. He ran the full length of the pitch in a diagonal line and scored a try on the opposite side. This lives in my memory as the first and best try I ever saw.

☐ I saw Whitehaven's first game in 1948 and stood outside the pavilion to shake hands with every player. They felt as tough as teak. Like everybody in this town, I'm Rugby daft. I was in London for two years, but felt back at home after ten minutes at a rugby ground.

☐ You know how some things just aren't meant to be, no matter what. Even when the physical odds are overcome, fate takes control and re-loads the dice. It was like that for Northern at Wigan. We could't win there and I'm talking about the days when Wigan were still fielding human beings.

My tale begins on a Friday night in winter and it was Wigan away. There were loads of good reasons for not going, the main one being, I didn't want to go. Night trips into Lancashire had long since lost their appeal, if they'd ever had any in the first place. Too many dashed hopes, I suppose. On this, at least, it seemed the players shared my reluctance for these excursions since on nearly every occasion one or more would cry off and the team taking the field was never the one promised in the paper. Besides all that, this was winter, there was fog about and the M62 can be a fickle beast, and after all this was Wigan. We hadn't won there in forty-odd years and form this season didn't suggest anything would change that night.

We discussed all this, my dad, my sister and myself, none of us too keen, but eventually deciding to go, reasoning that it was better to be there than fretting at home. Watching or waiting, each was depressing that season. It was a night out and you never knew, maybe after forty-odd years we were due a win. This was all arranged before we really appreciated just how some things cannot be. That night fate decided to teach us the principle and make sure we never raised false hopes again. It was a night to remember all right.

We paid for a parking spot only to find ample free parking much closer to the ground as we approached. No matter. It was all forgotten as the match began and, for a change, Northern had decided to make a game of it. Two breakaway tries from Les Sellers put them in control and we were congratulating ourselves on having made the right decision. This was to be a night to talk about, forty-odd years of history wiped away, and we were there to see it.

Half-time approached and Northern were in no danger. Wigan were having an off night. The mist was swirling about, but I could see enough to feel pretty confident. During the interval the mist became thick fog. In a few minutes you couldn't see the pitch, let alone the far side of the ground. The ref had no option but to call off the game. Utterly deflated we wandered back to the car to begin the journey home. That the fog was back to a light mist but a few hundred yards from Central Park was enough to make you wild.

Back on the M62, just at that spot where the white rose is on the plaque, the car packed in. Not a peep. The dice were well and truly loaded against us. The AA took over two hours to find us and it was a long, cold night.

Northern didn't win the re-arranged game and I gave up ever expecting to see my team win at Wigan. When they can call on such forces to help, I say, give 'em the points. I'll settle for getting home at a reasonable hour: you won't catch me questioning the inevitable.

☐ We had a really bad spell of weather in 1963. I think Hunslet went twelve weeks without a league game. We were to play Rochdale Hornets on the first Saturday in February, but every time it thawed it froze again, and with a ground like Rochdale's Athletic Ground with its Pennine backdrop, the chances of it thawing out were not good.

A lot of people won't know this, but it states in the Rugby League bye-laws that the Secretary of the home team can call off a game if he thinks the field is unfit for play.

On the Saturday morning I was up at Parkside, waiting for a call from the Rochdale Secretary . A man who was walking his dog on the cinder track shouted over to me. 'Is it on?'

'I don't know yet', I shouted back, 'It's up to the home Secretary.'

He was outraged. 'Bloody Government! Are they sticking their noses into Rugby League now!'

☐ I'm not sure whether this falls under aromatherapy but I suppose there must be some professor somewhere who, at this very moment in time, is carrying out experiments in his laboratory on the effects of smells on the human brain. I say this because one particular aroma has the remarkable effect on me of triggering the recall of a past event.

One whiff from the professor's bottle labelled 'Fragrance of freshly cut grass with essence of early evening kick-off in August', and immediately I'd be back at a sun-drenched Parkside circa 1964, shortly after Bradford Northern had reformed. There is hardly anything of that game I could tell you about, but what I do remember is the sensation of the pollen, or whatever it was, hitting my sinuses as I entered the stand paddock near the pavilion at Parkside.

Parkside - 'The finest green sward that Rugby League has ever been played on' - as I seem to remember it once described. Parkside and another balmy afternoon in early season; and my catching a ball, the real leather match ball, which had been kicked into touch by 'Old' Northern's New Zealand full back, Bill Seddon: and everyone around me, behind the big white picket fencing, shouting 'Get the lad signed on, Hunslet,' as I threw the ball back to the wingman who was immaculately kitted out in the Parksiders famous myrtle, white and flame.

I gave some thought to having one of those scented rub-offs, the sort you find with the perfume ads in the Sunday Colour Mags, inserted into my *Grounds of Rugby League* book, just for the atmosphere. Of course it would have had to be a universal smell with which most Rugby League supporters could have identified, and I could think of only one which epitomised the game and the grounds of Rugby League. As that smell is wintergreen it is perhaps fortunate that I took the idea no further.

☐ Rugby League was first played at Elland Road in 1938. The Championship Final was between Leeds and Hunslet and they were due to play at Belle Vue, Wakefield. Sir Edwin Airey, who was Chairman at Leeds at the time, said it was daft to take the game to another town. Playing at a soccer ground had never been heard of then. They paid £500 to play there. When you think about all that time ago when the communications were relatively unsophisticated, no fax, no telephones hardly, it was a marvellous job they did to organise it in a few days and over 54,000 turned up.

☐ With fifteen minutes to go before kick-off at the old Craven Park, Hull Kingston Rovers were a player short, an out of town winger who usually travelled from the West Riding by train

and then took a taxi to the ground. The telephone rang in the Secretary's office and the winger announced sheepishly that he had caught the wrong train and was ringing from Bridlington station, some 30 miles away.

'What should I do now sir?' he enquired nervously. 'Well lad, if I were you I'd bugger off home,' was the reply from the Secretary before he slammed down the phone.

☐ I started watching Rugby League by chance in December 1960. I used to read the Blackpool 'Green' Sports edition on a Saturday night from cover to cover. I'd started playing Rugby at grammar school and the Rugby League sports pages just captured my interest.

I went with a school mate to watch Blackpool Borough play Workington Town at the old St Anne's Road Greyhound Stadium on a cold December day. I'd never seen such big blokes playing any sport before. Two things attracted me immediately: the raw aggression on the field and the friendliness and good humour of the crowd. I've been hooked on the game ever since. It was all so different from league soccer at Bloomfield Road. Blackpool FC were a big club then with Stan Matthews still in the side. The Rugby League players struck me as real people like your own dad - fans talked to them by name. I couldn't believe it when Brian Bevan joined Blackpool for their last season at the 'dog track'. Bev never seemed to like playing on the narrow pitch. The inside rail for the greyhound hare was right up to the touchline and a good sliding tackle would put a winger underneath it. Van Vollenhoven and Jan Prinsloo of St. Helens suffered that fate!

☐ From our back yard about one and a half miles away I'd hear the roar of the crowd. Sometimes I'd be part of that crowd, when Grandad would call and say, 'Get thisen ready. We're off t'match.' A quick change and off we'd go. First stop the Jolly Sailor at the bottom of Heath Common, then on to the match, into the ground and waiting in anticipation for the teams.

I can remember at the time enjoying Grandad's cryptic comments as much as the match. When Rocky would try a penalty kick for touch, Grandad would say, 'What the devil's Turner taking t'kick for?' Well Rocky's kick would go far but not find touch and Grandad would grumble, 'Aye, I knew that would happen.'

He was the only person I know who could carry on conversation with someone, watch the match and me as well. If ever I turned away to study the crowd's reaction, there'd be a tap on my shoulder and a gruff voice saying, 'Sithee, I've paid for thee to watch t'match, not t'crowd.'

☐ A lot of people might wonder why Hull F.C. fans sing *Old Faithful*. It started in the mid 1930s, when an American cowboy song by Gene Autrey was popular in this country. Hull F.C.'s captain Joe Oliver was nicknamed *The points machine* at the time and at one match the crowd spontaneously began singing the ballad *Old Faithful* in his honour and it has been the club's battle hymn ever since.

☐ In the sixties I can recall the Aussies playing at Warrington and the crowd chanting, 'Eddie Waring for Vietnam!' I think a lot of Northerners didn't like the way he portrayed our lives.

☐ In the 1950s I played for Keighley. At that time there was a lot of personal contact with the crowd. It was part of the excitement at Odsal, where you came out of the clubhouse at the top and had to walk 150 yards to the pitch. The referee and players after the match usually had a police escort and the crowd were able to shout abuse, but I never heard of any players getting attacked. It was similar at Batley when we used to change in the old cricket pavilion and had to walk across the cricket field before running out onto the field. At Lawkholme we used to have to walk from the wooden hut, and spectators would let on if they knew you personally.

A professional player's got to get a buzz out of playing. He doesn't only do it for money. Every player has to go out there and perform and be admired, and he gets a lift from spectators and the atmosphere. What they seem to have done now is take the players away from the crowd - they come out of a hole and go back into a hole. They're that well guarded with stewards and police that you can't get near them. You've paid good money to go and see the players but you're given very little contact with them. It's like going horse racing and not being able to see the horses parading around.

☐ Well, did he bloody score? There were three or four of us who always met behind the left-hand goal post at the Wheldon Road end of the ground. A study of the programme generally included one A N Other. The buzz around the ground was that he was a Scottish Union player down for a trial. Hawick seemed to be the favourite place and we once had a name, 'Black.'

I remember the ground being shrouded in a cocktail of mist from the River Aire and home coal fire smog from the rows of terraced houses which stretched down Wheldon Road to Fryston. On a good day the steam trains from York would linger, waiting to enter Castleford station. Since the line was just beyond the

opposite end of the ground you could guarantee that when Mick McManus was asked to do his party piece the train would move off. He would pick up the ball ten yards out from the line and with what appeared to be the whole of the opposing side strung around his neck like some giant clothes horse, he would disappear into the pall of black smoke belched from the train as it started to pull away. The cry from our end of the ground would go up, 'Well, did he bloody score?'

My halcyon days came to an end when at eighteen I went to work in London. Living in the South and South Wales, I was dependent on the late Eddie Waring to keep me in touch with Rugby League. Since returning to Yorkshire I have decided to visit Wheldon Road again. Who knows who I will find behind the left-hand post? I wonder, is the sacred spot still marked from which Arthur Atkinson kicked a goal from about seventy yards out?

☐ One of the strangest incidents I was ever involved in as a spectator was while watching a Blackpool Borough v Dewsbury game in 1961 at St Anne's Road Stadium. I went to the match with some school mates. We tied some in Blackpool's colours to a metal stanchion on the popular side cover. The referee stopped the game until we climbed up and untied the balloons. He said they were distracting him - he was mistaking them for the touch judge's flag. The local paper reported the incident in the match report. I kept the paper cutting for years!

☐ The 1930s were synonymous with poverty, hardship and mass unemployment, with children walking the streets of Widnes in their bare feet.

One of the Widnes players told me that he pawned his suit to go to Wembley. George, the pawnbroker, offered him 25/- but after the player told him he was going to Wembley, he let him have another five bob.

Even our heroes had suffered hardship. McCue and Shannon would travel half price on the buses to save a few coppers - wearing old school caps. But one day all the misery and gloom somehow vanished. The tall chimneys in Ditton Road and West Bank and Dennis's 202 foot chimney stopped belching smoke.

Widnes were at Wembley - the little chemical town. People were so happy because their team of thirteen local lads were playing at Wembley - something which will probably never be repeated.

It was just on 3pm. I was a sad and disillusioned young man for I could not raise the 10/6d for the train fare from Farnworth Station.

I had seen hundreds of people on their way to London. Some on bikes, some on the back of a lorry and any vehicle which was roadworthy. Widnes, including the buses, shops and cinemas, was literally covered with black and white. There was bunting across the streets and all the characters had come out, including the ever-so-jolly chimney sweep.

A kind-hearted man from Timperley's cake shop had brought forms and chairs from his shop and put a wireless on the wall. Among those listening was a chap with one arm. He had left the other hanging on the barbed wire at Dardanelles. It would appear a well-known bookmaker from Newtown had given him odds of 100 - 1, saying Widnes had no chance. You can imagine the excitement as the game came to its finish.

'We are now in the final seconds of the game. The score is 10 - 3 and Van Rooyen has got the ball. The game is over and Widnes have won the Cup!'

The man with the one arm and two quart bottles of Stingo in his pocket was standing on the end of the form and when the final whistle went everybody was jumping up and down in celebration. Consequently the form gave way. He finished on the floor shouting, 'A hundred to bloody one!'

I went to see my heroes when they came back to the Town Hall to a rapturous welcome from thousands of Widnesians.

It is said Widnes gave Wigan £100 for George Van Rooyen, who ranks among the Chemics' all-time greats. The stories about his strength are legendary in Widnes and he is supposed to have swum across the Mersey after missing the Transporter car.

One day they played Warrington and as they were scrumming down, one of the Wire forwards called George some unprintable name. Van Rooyen knocked the forward out stone cold and then walked up to the referee and said, 'The name is Van Rooyen,' and promptly walked off the field of play!

☐ The day was Sunday, March 17th 1968, and history was in the making in cold, wet Huddersfield. What, you may wonder, could be on the cards? Sunday Rugby was the answer! For the first time Fartown was to be the scene of a professional Rugby League game being played on the Sabbath and a Challenge Cup tie to boot. Father and I sat squashed in the stand soaking up the atmosphere. Up pops the *Yorkshire Evening Post* reporter and asks father's opinion on the match. 'T'gate'll be 'alved by t'weather,' was his learned response.

The tension mounted as 18,500 fans waited in anticipation of what promised to be a titanic struggle. They screamed with delight as the claret and gold gladiators strutted out confidently having dispatched St. Helens and Halifax in previous rounds. The suspense was unbearable as the two protagonists locked in battle. The half-time whistle came, promptly followed by a mass pitch invasion. Finally, the ultimate was achieved as the Fartowners were through to the semis for the first time in six years.

How could I celebrate the best Rugby League moment in my short fifteen year life? Give my rattle some stick, thinks I! The corncrake-like sound echoed in my ears as my heart pounded with elation. Suddenly the sound subsided as I witnessed the end of the rattle take off vertically. As if in slow motion it pirouetted Nureyev-style in the air. The rattle showed no respect for the occasion as it hurtled towards my father's prominent proboscis, striking it a lusty blow. Father, showing his usual restraint, spluttered, 'What the 'ell do you think you're doing, you bloody idiot!' Somewhat shocked at the sight of his mutilated nose, I immediately forgot the joy of the victory.

I escorted my wounded father from the scene, only to be confronted by a human mountain in the form of one of my father's friends.

'Who's thumped you Bernard? I'll get 'im,' he bawled.

'Nobody, it's this silly sod here,' he replied, thrusting an accusing digit in my direction. Somewhat crestfallen we returned home, father bloodied but victorious. He still bears the scar to this day.

☐ A few steps down the terracing was a lone, extremely vociferous and self-opinionated Bramley fan with plenty of interesting advice to players, officials and visiting supporters. My two neighbours were highly delighted, saying that they hadn't seen 'the man who stopped Lionel Cooper' at recent games. They swore it was a true story but it may be apocryphal.

Years previously our hero had been, in his opinion, a star performer for Bramley Rugby Union Club's third XV. For some reason he had incurred the displeasure of his team mates who collectively decided to do something about him. They enlisted the aid of a friend who was well known in amateur Rugby League circles. He told the Bramley coaching staff of this wonderful prospect languishing in the Rugby Union Club's third XV. As a result our hero played his one and only professional game for Bramley 'A'.

Eventually, whether out of pity on Bramley's part I know not, he got the job of sponge and bucket man to the 'A' team where he became well known for his altercations with opposing fans.

The end of his career came one Saturday afternoon when he was temporarily promoted to first team duty for a game against Huddersfield. With more than the usual number of opposing fans to argue with he became more and more excited as the game wore on. The climax came late in the game when Bramley, many points adrift, were enjoying a rare spell in Huddersfield's 25. The end of this spell came when the legendary Australian winger, Lionel Cooper, intercepted a stray Bramley pass and sped majestically down the wing for a certain try. However, as he passed the Bramley dug-out, he came crashing to the ground felled by a bucket thrust between his ankles. Naturally officialdom took a dim view of this happening and thus ended the Rugby League career of 'the man who stopped Lionel Cooper.

□ We had spent a glorious weekend in the Dales and I was very reluctant to get back into normal routine. In the car, as I approached Otley, I realised that my timing was such that I would be getting to Featherstone shortly before kick-off and that they had a home match. In the car with me were Tam and Abi, who was only eighteen months old. I had seen babies, toddlers and frail old grannies and grandads happily attending Rugby League matches. I wouldn't have dared to take a toddler to soccer.

So we went to the match and Abi peered through the bars and within minutes was screaming for our team. I remember little of the match itself. It was the occasion that grabbed me, the identity of crowd with team and most of all, the identity of crowd with crowd. And that included opposition supporters and our supporters alike, sharing their love of the occasion, their love of the game and their passion for their own team, many of whom were personally well known to them, local lads who they saw in the street daily. Plenty of banter, but never personal animosity. It was then I could sense that Rugby League played such a major part in the cultural life of these communities, a part that professional soccer could never aspire to.

I love music, opera and theatre, but none of them can quite match that sense of shared experience. And culture is essentially about groups - communities.

□ We once went to Blackpool for a club's weekend outing. On the last morning the landlady noticed one of the beds had been broken and wanted not the money to cover the repair cost for the bed but the full cost of a new one, so the lads had a whip round to pay for the bed. On giving the landlady the agreed amount the lads then said they would be taking the old

bed as they had paid for it. The landlady, after moaning on and on, then called the police. The policeman heard both sides then walked away saying, 'They've paid for the bed. Its theirs.' Four of our players ran upstairs and carried off the bed and mattress to the waiting coach.

□ Rochdale Hornets were on the way home from an away game against Hull K.R. back in 1958. We stopped off in York and in the same hotel were Hull F.C. players who had been playing over in Lancashire that day.

While both sets of players were mixing socially, it came on the radio that Hull had been drawn to play Rochdale Hornets in the first round of the RL Challenge Cup. At that time Hull had an almost invincible pack - Mick Scott, Tommy Harris, the Drake twins and Johnny Whiteley. Our Jim Parr was stood behind Tommy Harris, who was heard to say, 'The bloody scoreboard won't be big enough!'

Anyway, Hornets went over the week after, and to everyone's surprise knocked Hull out of the cup. In the players' bar after the match, Jim Parr went over to Tommy Harris and asked, 'How's your scoreboard going on Tommy?' You can imagine Tommy's reply, but it was all taken in good spirit. They went on to beat Bradford and York in the next rounds, just falling at mighty Wigan, 5 - 3 in the semi-final.

On the trawlers we went to Bear Island, Greenland, Murmansk and Iceland. We'd be out about twenty one days: if it got to twenty two we worried a bit. The lads always shoved a *Sports Mail* in with their gear and the skippers telephoned for the results. That was when eight ships a day landed at Hull. They used to announce over the tannoy at the Boulevard which ships were home.

During the war I was stationed at Guyotville, a place just west of Algiers. We marched up to the main building, a huge white post office, and standing right in the middle of the road directing traffic was the great Gus Risman, or Sergeant Gus Risman as he now was. Funny things happen like that in Rugby League. I once came across the well known Jazz trumpeter Dizzy Gillespie when I was in France with Jack MacNamara.

When I was in the Merchant Navy, tuning in to the BBC World Service was a must. Being in the Sydney Cricket Ground to see a game was like a pilgrim in Jerusalem. But finding the results in an Egyptian newspaper in the late 60s was one of the great thrills.

Eddie Waring went out to Australia on the *Indomitable* in 1946. He took a cine camera with him and when he came back he edited it and showed it round to supporters. I think he charged twelve guineas a time. Eddie was forward thinking, he had big ideas on spreading the game.

I was once in the Conservative Club near Wembley. I got talking to a refined middle-aged couple who looked at the clock as it was coming up to three and said, 'We'll have to go now. We always listen to Eddie Waring while we're taking our tea.' Eddie had that kind of impact.

The bitter sweet story of Rugby League
A career in the game

In my younger days we had a real keen physiotherapist at St. Helens. A great bloke, but he insisted on giving us all a wintergreen massage after training. He was good, but very strong. We'd let the forwards go first, hoping that he'd be knackered by the time it was our turn. One day me and my mate decided to give the ordeal a miss and get straight off to the pictures. I grabbed a shower, had a quick towel down and that was that.

Ten minutes into the film and my balls started to tingle. Another ten minutes and they were on fire. I'd only dried myself down on the towel that the physio had been wiping his wintergreened hands on all morning!

I went to the bog, but with people wandering in and out, I couldn't really hoist my knackers under the cold tap. It was my mate who came up with the idea of cooling me off.

That's how I found myself watching the film with two Lyons Maid orange lollies melting in my underpants. It did the job, but I had all on explaining to my mum how I'd arrived home with wet orange underpants.

I met Brian Rose who played for Whitehaven, on a trip to Wembley one year. We were all having a drink and getting on well with the Whitehaven party who were staying in our hotel in Harrow. One said to me, 'Have you ever been to Whitehaven, lad?' and I said, 'Aye, many times.'

I'll always remember our winger Norman Brelsford about 1972, scoring five tries in a match up there, but four of them were handed to him on a plate by his centre, the great Frank Myler, who despite being at the tail-end of his career could still turn it on. My Whitehaven buddy, pointing to a man at the bar, said, 'Go have a word with Brian Rose. He played in that match.'

So I went up to him, and got talking about Wembley, but when I mentioned Brelsford's five tries, Brian got agitated.

'Are you trying to spoil my weekend? Seventeen years on and that game still haunts me.'

He went on to tell me he was a strapping young lad at the time, brimming with confidence. When he went to the ground and looked at the team sheet, he saw he was up against Frank Myler and thought, 'No problem.'

'The rest you know' he said. 'For four of the tries Myler came straight through me and left me like a rag doll on the ground. When I walked off the pitch that day, I left it a much wiser nineteen year old.'

☐ Team spirit is the major factor in the success of a club. And that doesn't mean you're just playing with twelve other guys. A lot of coaches these days try to emulate a nice social environment and encourage social acceptance. Taking the wives to the local Chinese restaurant is part of that.

☐ When schools went comprehensive it was a blow for Rugby League. The comprehensive schools switched to Rugby Union because that's what grammar schools had played.

☐ When I was at Ashton Road School I used to love all sport, gymnastics, athletics, the lot. The games master was Roy Close and he warned us that if we forgot our PE gear we'd get a crack. I got my days mixed up, forgot my stuff and had to take my place in line with all the skivers to get walloped. I could take that. What I couldn't take was when he came up to me later in the playground, put his arm round my shoulders and said, 'I know what happened, Malcolm.' I knew what had happened as well. Since that time I have found little trouble motivating myself in sport. Although it was pure accident how I came to be a Rugby League player. I was playing soccer. The match was called off and so I jumped on the rugby coach to Hunslet.

☐ I hated PE at school. All my reports said, 'Claire needs more gusto.' I hated netball, I hated hockey. They never let us have a go at Rugby. Now I coach Smawthorne Panthers Under 8s. I did my Level 1 Coaching Certificate at Morley and now I'm booked in for Level 2. At first these little lads used to come up to me and say, 'But you're a girl.' I soon put them through their paces.

☐ In a playground when you're a kid, a boy is given a ball and so he learns how to throw and pass; a girl is given a skipping rope. Boys get a head start. That's why women have a problem reading the game of Rugby at first, because they haven't been given the opportunity to learn. But we don't turn round and say, 'You're shit!' when they first come because a woman has a different temperament to a man and they might not come again.

The first thing I dropped when I left school was sport. I was fourteen stone and wore those big blue knickers and the teachers made me do things I didn't want to do. By the time I was twenty six I started doing aerobics and enjoyed it. Then I started playing women's Rugby League. I've got two children and a full time job, but all my social life revolves round Rugby League. If somebody said to me, 'You can't play no more,' I'd be lost.

☐ My career really took a turn when I sat down one day and thought about where I was going with Rugby League. I knew exactly where I would be next week, even next month on a given day. I was more adventurous. Castleford didn't believe me, but I decided to emigrate to Australia and play over there. I packed in my job at Ledston Luck pit, packed two bags and jumped on the aeroplane at Leeds. When I landed at Mascot airport in Sydney there were three cameras from three different television stations waiting for me. Jim Comans, a solicitor, had acted as my agent after I'd been on the 1970 tour and he fixed it for me to play for Manly Warringah.

There was no comparison between Cas and Manly. Now I was on the Pacific Ocean with lovely palm trees outside my window. I could have Chateaubriand stuffed with oysters for dinner, previously I'd been used to two oysters on the sea front at Scarborough.

The clubhouse at Manly had a turnover of 1.8 million dollars in 1971, from the poker machines and gambling . The physical demands of the game were totally different. In the early 70s every man, woman and their dog went jogging in Australia. I went down to the local surf club with the coach, Ron Willey, and I had all on keeping up with men in their sixties.

☐ When the Australians came for me I was working on a building site in Harrogate. Bruce Wellesden and Wally Ward came onto the site and whipped me over to the Dragonara Hotel in Leeds. I was filthy and I walked into the restaurant with my work boots on. They wanted me to sign for Penrith, but I didn't think there was any way Dewsbury would let me go. Two days later at Crown Flatt my suspicions were confirmed. I was asked into the boardroom and told that Dewsbury were building their team around me. They then told the two Aussies that, 'Our Captain is not being released'. I came out of the room and then an extraordinary thing happened. The Dewsbury board, possibly thinking they would scare the Aussies off, asked for the then unheard of figure of £20,000 for me. Without batting an eyelid the Aussies signed a cheque, nipped it out of the book and handed it over. My wage in 1973 as a plumber was £1,300 a year. I didn't ask for a transfer but the following Wednesday I was signed by Penrith. Later that week somebody phoned me from London and told me that Penrith had lost 70 points to 7 to Manly and had finished as wooden spoonists in the Australian League. In less than a week I had moved from the British champions to the bottom club in Australia. When I finally arrived down under I was given no illusions about the job ahead of me. Out of thirty players in the dressing room when I arrived, only two said 'hello' to me.

☐ When Tom came over from South Africa, he couldn't speak a word of English. That didn't last long though, six months later he was the biggest yarn spinner at the club. We'd all heard the rumour that he was paid all year round and I was a bit pissed off about it. After brooding on it for a while, I decided to go and confront the board. On my way up the stairs I met Tom coming down and decided to ask him whether it was true about him being paid summer and winter. He looked me straight in the eye and said, 'Spud, no.'

On my way down, I bumped into Leonie, his wife. 'Oh yes,' she said, 'Tom loves it here. He gets everything he wants. You know he gets paid summer and winter.'

Bloody charming, that was enough for me. When I went to complain to the board about it, one of them said, 'You're not trying to tell us that you're as good as him.'

'I am in chuffing summer,' I said.

☐ The chap that signed me at Castleford committed suicide a week after. I'd come straight out of amateur football into the first team and after the first two of three games in which I didn't play so well somebody said, 'No wonder he committed suicide if he signed this bloke on!'

☐ On Christmas Day 1944 I scored a try to help Dewsbury YMCA win the Challenge Cup at Barley Mow in the old Leeds and District League Under 18s section.

On the Boxing Day I went to our local derby match, Batley versus Dewsbury at Mount Pleasant. I paid through the turnstile and took my place on the long stand to await the start of the game. Soon Lawrie Scott, a local amateur player and Rugby League reporter, came to me.

'John,' he said, 'Dewsbury are a player short and want you to play for them.'

I went to the dressing room, signed an agreement to play a total of six games on trial to be reviewed and then played left wing to the famous Australian Centre, Vic Hey. What a thrill for a seventeen year old. Although I was scared at first, I'm pleased to say that neither my nerves nor my earlier Christmas lunch affected my play.

The Dewsbury directors later came to interview me at the YMCA hostel and offered me £100 to sign for them. I turned them down. I later signed on for Batley for £150, paid in three instalments, and no back-hander! I played 343 times for Batley before they sold me to Oldham for £2,650.

☐ A lot of Welsh lads came north in the 1930s because of the poverty. When Oliver Morris came up to Hunslet in 1937 he was a sensation. I think he was the best stand-off half I ever saw. There was a very famous administrator at Warrington called Bob Anderton. He was the first to notice him. He said, 'There's a lad playing with Pontypridd. We thought about signing him but we've decided he's too small.' Oliver was only nine stone six. We sent two scouts down one Saturday and they decided to sign him, but they had to see his father first. The father was a fire-breathing Primitive Methodist with a big moustache. He wouldn't accept a cheque so Hunslet had to send four hundred and fifty one pound notes down to the local Midland Bank.

When Oliver got here I remember Billy Hannah, the well-known Cumbrian trainer, saying, 'I see you've bought another bloody whippet.'

☐ Leeds were always impressed by Oliver Morris. He once played opposite the big strapping stand-off Vic Hey who was 15 stone-odd and Oliver continually fetched him down in clouds of dust. Towards the end of 1939 Hunslet needed money so they agreed to let him go to Leeds. It was a very peculiar deal: £1000 or £500 if the war didn't start by October 1st. The war clouds gathered and gathered and it all broke out when Oliver had only played two peacetime matches. Oliver was posted to Cairo after he joined up. He wanted to be an officer and he ended up with a Welsh regiment in Palestine. He told me, 'It's great. All we do is play Rugby all over the Middle East.' I told him it wouldn't last. Oliver got posted to Italy and was killed in the Gothic Line in 1944.

☐ The old man wanted to get away from Wales. He had been offered terms to play with Tottenham Hotspur but a week later Salford signed him and paid him £8 a game. That was in the 30s. I suppose it was natural that our Bev and me should follow in his steps and become Rugby League players. Bev will tell you that in all his years playing he never got angry, but I know one time when he did. I was six or seven and he was fourteen. I gave him a dig on the nose and he chased me round the house. The old man was the peacemaker that day.

☐ Throughout its history the famous Travellers Saints nursery in Featherstone has produced an outstanding array of professional players. Top clubs such as Leeds, Hull, Hull K.R., Castleford and particularly Featherstone have regularly raided the prolific production line.

The conveyor belt continues to run smoothly judging by the fact that no less than five youngsters have during the 1992-93 season been recruited by Featherstone Rovers. This is of particular significance to me, as I know there should almost certainly have been a sixth - my son - Steven.

Steve's initiation into the world of Rugby League was as a two-week-old baby at Post Office Road. By the time he was eleven months he amazed everyone through his outstanding ability to talk fluently. I will never forget the astonishment on the faces of several Post Office Road faithfuls when a player dropped the ball. Steven, a babe-in-arms, shouted 'Knock on'. It may seem incredible but it's true. 'He's been here before' exclaimed a perplexed lady supporter.

She may have been right too, as at the age of only seven Steve was made captain of the Travellers Under 9s, a role he was to retain through the grades of 11s and 13s. His understanding of the game and outstanding ability to organise and dictate play impressed everyone who saw him. He had the game well and truly in his pocket, so much so that county selection was almost automatic.

Steven was a pupil at Sharlston Junior School, another traditionally famous provider to the great game. Here, again, his leadership qualities gained him the team captaincy.

In January 1986 the *Yorkshire Evening Post* revealed that Wakefield Schools and St. Helens were to contest the Under 11s curtain raiser to the Wembley Challenge Cup Final. Several trial games were to be held in the Wakefield area, culminating in tears of joy in the Mullaney household as coach Andy Stacey named Steven to lead the side at the Twin Towers. The excitement was enhanced still further with the news that the BBC were going to televise the match for the very first time.

Wakefield won convincingly by 17 points to 0 after a fine team performance including a try by Steven Mullaney which captured the hearts of millions of TV viewers when, unable to contain his joy, he burst into to tears in full view of the cameras. The BBC switchboards were inundated with calls to re-run the match which they did the next day on *Sunday Grandstand*. Alex Murphy predicted a fine future for many of the players but seemed to take a particular shine to Steve. Perhaps he could see something of himself in the little scrum half.

On 18th September 1987, Steven was struck by a car while he was on his way home from school. He suffered severe head injuries and was never to recover. Two days later he died in Pinderfields Hospital, Wakefield. The moment the doctor tells you that your child is going to die is the start of a terrible nightmare. No parents can ever accept the fact that they have outlived their children. It is the worst thing that can ever happen to anyone. The injustice of it all eats you away.

That's when Featherstone Rovers came to the rescue. The club had never operated a lottery or club shop or anything like that on a professional scale before, but with the advent of the contract system it was a must.

The Chairman at that time, Richard Evans, who had helped the family a great deal after Steven's death had said that he thought I was the man for the job, if I was prepared to take the considerable risk. I cast my mind back to the words that Steven said after his moment of glory at Wembley: 'Thanks Dad, I wouldn't have been playing at Wembley if you hadn't helped me. The next time I'm here I will be captain of Rovers.'

My mind was instantly made up. In my view the public of Featherstone were robbed of a great deal of pleasure when Steven was taken. I had been given a new challenge and purpose in life, a chance to replace as much as possible of that pleasure by providing the financial resources to secure a healthy future for the club.

The response was beyond belief. From nothing the club now rakes in around £150,000 per annum from the lottery and shop and that in a village where only 11,000 people are over the age of 18. Many big town clubs are envious of such off- the-field success, which would not exist but for the inspiration given to me by my son.

Steven's Wembley photo has pride of place at the Rovers headquarters and the boys' match at Wembley is now the Steven Mullaney Memorial match. In his short life he achieved much. Rovers have a lot to thank him for.

Till We Have Built Jerusalem

Leaving a terraced house for a semi-detached

Moving on

☐ We employed a young choreographer to unsettle the Aussies at the beginning of the World Cup Final at Wembley. We took the theme of the 1812 Overture. The choreographer wanted to play the tune as the players walked out of the tunnel to the halfway line and then let the cannons go off. But I thought we could out-psyche the Aussies better if we put loudspeakers in the tunnel and hit them with *Jerusalem*. The last time we played *Land of Hope and Glory*, but it reminds me of the Hurray Henrys too much. Besides *Jerusalem* contains the line 'chariots of fire' and it stimulates the crowd as much as the players. You can imagine how intimidated the Aussies must have felt: a World Cup Final at Wembley with nearly 80,000 partisans singing *Jerusalem* at them.

☐ I have read a poem by J B Priestley which describes Northern men in their overcoats and mufflers walking past gasworks walls on their way to a Rugby League match. It talks about their proud jutting jaws and stout stocky bodies, their grit and their determination. Well that's all well and good, but it's not got much to do with Rugby League fans these days. If I look out of my window when there's a match on, I see kids in Nike trainers and fifty quid replica jerseys of their favourite club. They join in when Tina

---

And did those feet in ancient time,
Walk upon England's mountains green?
And was the holy lamb of God
On England's pleasant pastures seen?
And did the countenance divine
Shine forth upon our clouded hills?
And was Jerusalem builded here
Among those dark satanic mills?

Turner sings *Simply the Best* over the stadium tannoy system and they haven't got a flat cap between them to throw in the air when somebody scores a try.

☐ For all that I'm proud of the northern way of life, I have to say I am bitterly disappointed with the way former administrators of the Rugby League have behaved. We relied on the local butcher, the baker, men whose interests went no further than the signposts into the next town. We have suppressed the game ourselves and that's why it didn't move anywhere in eighty-five years. There is a tradition to keep, the loyalty, the honesty, the cleanliness of the sport. My old granny used to say 'No peas above sticks'. In Australia they call it the tall poppy syndrome. We need to keep that. You don't get top players in this game sneaking through a side door and into a Porsche. They come out of a bath and have a drink with the fans. That's the kind of egalitarianism I want to keep. That and the simplicity of love in sport.

☐ Rugby League is a northern game with solid roots in the North. It can be linked to the community, to our industry, to our attitudes and to our way of life. This is why it is so popular amongst northern people. What puzzles me is why the powers that be want to implant the game in areas such as London and Wales and Kent, places which have their own cultures and their own sports which reflect them, places where our game has no roots. What is the underlying purpose of these short-sighted excursions? I would love to be a fly on the wall when a Jehovah's Witness comes knocking on a Rugby League development person's door. 'We know a better life and we would like you to share it, we are going to build a Kingdom Hall in your back garden.' Unless these Witnesses could convince our development people that it would lead to bigger sponsorship deals then the dogs would be out and they'd be scampering off down the path.

We need to develop the game in our own area, strengthen the smaller clubs so there is more competition. If other people like what we have, then by all means give them encouragement and support, let them develop the game. Professional clubs appearing in barren Rugby League areas, with instant access to the major leagues just because they have got some money, is a nonsense. Mighty oaks may from little acorns grow, but they don't do it overnight.

☐ Sometimes we are disadvantaged by the very name of places Rugby League is played at. Ascot and Virginia Water have a better ring to them than Wigan and Barrow.

☐ The facilities at Rugby League grounds need to improve. It is not enough to offer people a soggy hot dog and a wall to piss against. Unfortunately the game is still played in slum conditions. You can't go on blaming poverty and the recession.

☐ Not so long ago we commissioned a survey from a PhD student at Liverpool. He went round the grounds asking people about watching Rugby League. He wanted to know if they were happy sitting on a bit of bloody board, no glass in the windows and the bloody rain coming down. On the whole, people don't want uplifting, they want to do what their fathers and grandfathers did.

I was born in Thwaite Gate, Hunslet. It was the biggest parish in England and everybody there loved their Rugby, but they all had their own way of going about it. You had the dichotomy of two men living in the same street, going to the same match at the same time and dividing at the top of the street - stubborn about which way they went to the ground because that's the way their fathers had gone. Hull K.R. didn't think about that when they moved to a green-field site.

☐ When you cross North Bridge, you are in enemy territory. At one time you watched Hull if you were born in West Hull and Hull K.R. if you came from East Hull. When we pulled Hessle Road down a lot of families had to move to Bransholme Estate and the two rivals were forced to live next to each other for the first time. When a red and white marries a black and white in Hull, they call it a mixed marriage.

☐ There is a great sense of tradition in Huddersfield. After all it's where the game was born, but tradition doesn't win trophies. That's why the club's decision to move to Leeds Road was a good one. To do up Fartown and get rid of the weeds would have been far too costly. I know there is a school of thought that says every club has a right to its own stadium, but when you've a choice and it's pissing down, you'd be daft not to come in out of the rain.

The players have a right to their say as well and it said in the *Huddersfield Examiner* that they prefer Leeds Road so how can you argue against that? Another big facet in the renewing of Huddersfield is Alex Murphy. He's been called a big-headed git in the past, but for me he's as sound as a pound.

☐ Fartown leaving home is like a family outgrowing its terraced house and moving to a semi-detached. Of course, you leave your sentiments and perhaps your heart at the old place, but you take with you your dreams and hopes into the new.

☐ When I was a kid and they were redeveloping the centre of Manchester I used to find it tiresome hearing the old bores in bus queues complaining that they'd pulled down an old tobacconist's or a row of whippet shops in favour of a slab of Poulson's concrete. A quarter of a century later, when I saw houses being built on the '25 line' at Swinton's Station Road ground, I understood what they were on about.

At about the spot where Neil Fox passed the ball to Swinton's own Johnny Stopford for the winger to give Great Britain a glorious if short-lived lead against Reg Gasnier's all-conquering Aussies in the first Test Match I ever went to in the mid 60s, a transistor radio was playing Radio One. Concrete was being mixed.

The building company had set up its site office at the Pendlebury Road end of the ground, the side from which we used to approach the stadium every Saturday. It's a sad admission to make but my father, who died six years ago, is rarely in my thoughts these days - perhaps it's a natural consequence of having children of your own - yet when I saw the site office I remembered vividly the first time he fished a shilling out of his pocket in that car park so I could go through the children's entrance, having grown too big to be lifted over the turnstiles. Such was the marvellous informality of rugby grounds in those days. I was probably about

fourteen at the time. I remembered my Uncle Ike pressing half a crown into my hand one week and telling me not to tell my dad. I remembered, as anybody who went to Station Road in the 60s would, a mad old man called Eric who used to stand on the terraces and subject the referee and the opposition players to an unprovoked, intemperate, continuous torrent of abuse and occasionally spit at them as they disappeared down the players' tunnel.

Now these are people, my dad included, I am ashamed to say, who I am not in the habit of thinking of. But the shock of the realisation that Swinton would never move back to Station Road brought all this flooding back. As Geoffrey Moorhouse once wrote, the sports fan's true emotional home is not the family house but where his team plays. This is where he grows up, where he experiences joy, anguish, despair; the home he inherits from his father and passes on to his sons and daughters. Your family may move house, but the team doesn't. Except Swinton have. Successive boards of directors have squandered transfer fee money, failed in crackpot schemes to raise more money, sacked coaches they should have retained, appointed others who should never have been taken on and finally they have had to sell the ground for a million pounds which has gone straight to the Bank.

So the team is still in trouble and a three bedroomed townhouse with full gas central heating is going up at the spot on the terraces where I stood on a warm summer's evening to see Swinton beaten 31 - 2 by Halifax in the championship play offs. I consoled myself with the thought that at a party that evening Beryl Davies might let me feel her tits.

All I am saying, I suppose, is that Station Road was a rugby ground and I was a boy growing up. But multiply that by four or five or twenty thousand and you cannot escape the conclusion that the custodians of so much emotional baggage really ought to have taken better care of it.

☐ I came to Rugby League from an earlier life in America as a fan of the New York Giants in American football. I was immediately converted by Rugby League for its pace, its demands on the variety of skills. Most of all, Rugby League was a friendly, family game - and I became part of the Eagles family. I was a happy man.

Then came the change, the despising of the weak stragglers, the bringing in of American style 'planning', the move towards a select game for a few strong teams strategically separated on maps, so many miles from each other. I tell you (as a former professional Town Planner) planning needs to be about people, and the fans of Rugby League are something else. Behind all that shouting are people who care about their teams, their players, and they are not going to be taken in by a lot of wrong-headed ideas about money and geography.

At Nottingham's last game, the rugby fans put aside their club loyalties and united in their support for the game itself. Rugby fans flocked from all over.

Nottingham's last day may have reached its climax at half-time. Some of us came out of the stadium to present some flowers I had brought to Mrs Tomlinson, mother of Paul, the owner/manager. I asked some of the fans to come out and make a semi-circle around Mrs Tomlinson when we presented the flowers.

When the moment came, at the half-time break, fans poured out and the flowers were presented in front of a backdrop of fans and all their scarves. I could see Sheffield, Halifax, Wigan, Widnes, Castleford, Batley and many others - browns and reds and yellows and blacks and blues.

When Nottingham finally scored, having come so close so often, the cheers were marvellous to hear. I couldn't cheer much because I was choked up. Then, at the end, the players were cheered and clapped and patted off the field and through the stands like the true champions they were.

You must get the foundations right
Spreading the word

☐ I don't want to be a politician, but there has been, to some extent still is, a social attitude to the north, to its accents and to its people from industrial backgrounds. To a lot of people, including Northerners who ought to know better, Rugby League epitomises what is the conception of northern life. This masks the great athletic ability people playing this game have. In the past the media, which after all are southern based, have consistently refused to show the quality of Rugby League and indeed northern life unless it had a quaint colloquialism with it. The media found a niche for a northern sport and stuck with it.

We are talking here about an extremely professional game with very senior international athletes. We are not talking about the inability of a northern game to spread to the rest of the country, but the fact that a lot of people outside the traditional areas are being denied access to it. Anybody who went to Wigan and lived with Ellery Hanley for a year and saw his training regime, saw what he puts himself through, would know they were in the presence of a major Olympian. Get behind the façade and you will see top English track and field stars like

Ade Mafe and David Grindley have trained at Wigan. They go in the gym, see the standard and stand there open mouthed.

☐ I never really cared about poor old Fulham, I occasionally went to see them when Chelsea were playing away. Their own fans tried but could never quite manage it. Once a year the Boat Race between Oxford and Cambridge went past their ground. The boats were rowed at about 5mph by two sets of privileged middle class tossers, not much of a spectator sport. Fulham fans though used to turn en masse away from the game and to watch the boats go by.

But poor old Fulham did something really exciting. They brought Rugby League to us Southerners. I went with some of my mates to the first game.

I remember nothing about the game except that there were large numbers of northern men laughing at us because we cheered at the wrong time. Bringing Rugby League to us lot was supposed to do wonders for the North/South divide but we didn't take too kindly to being laughed at by a bunch of superior Northerners.

I suppose I should now tell you how I have been hooked on the game ever since, but it isn't quite like that. The next game I saw was about twelve years later. I was talked into it by two friends from West Yorkshire. Respecting their judgement I found myself driving Ian and Harry to Bradford to see Featherstone fight a relegation battle. From the moment we set off in the car it pissed down and didn't stop all night. Featherstone got hammered and I got wet. To me it looked like one bunch of grown men were running into another bunch, or worse still, throwing each other down into the mud and then all piling on top of the one at the bottom.

Standing there with the rain dripping down my neck convinced me of two things. One that Osgood, Hudson and Cooke would always be my heroes. And secondly that northern men might not be that superior after all.

☐ I went to see Fulham play Wigan in their very first game at Craven Cottage. Since that time I have been to every match, home and away, including friendlies bar a couple. Up to Rugby League coming to the capital I had only seen three games of it, all Wembley Finals.

When we play up in Cumberland I get up at four in the morning, drive to Hammersmith station and get the six o'clock train from Kings Cross. I might take in a non-league soccer game at lunchtime if I hear there's one in the area and then go on to the Rugby. Each season I spend over £500 in train fares and then hotel bills, food and drink on top of that. I actually look forward to nice weekends in Batley! You may think I'm a sports fanatic. You would be right. I've also been a season ticket holder at Chelsea for 25 years and I go to watch London Welsh Rugby Union.

☐ I can never understand why Rugby League never caught on in Wales. When you think that there is a very similar social background down there to that in the North of England - coalmines, industry, working class love of sport. Yet they've stuck to Rugby Union. I suppose we can't complain. Over the years we have pinched some of their best players.

☐ Now purpose-built stadiums on the outskirts of towns are replacing the traditional grounds rooted firmly within a community. Look at Hull K.R., look at Ryedale York. At one time all you had to do on a Sunday morning was follow the crowd and you'd end up at a Rugby match. If you followed the crowd on a Sunday now you'd end up at a car boot sale, Argos or Do it All.

☐ I came originally from the North-East, so Rugby was not part of my upbringing. I was first introduced to the game while I was at university. I shared rooms with another woman who was from Hull. On Sundays we would go and do our washing together and then travel over to the Boulevard.

☐ If anything is worthwhile it takes time to build because you must get the foundations right. Anything that is going to be of benefit is not achieved overnight. Scarborough was a brand-new development area. We had great plans and could see the potential for development. That a club in its infancy was allowed to die was a bitter blow to me. We had established the game in the schools, I had players in training from the North-East and we were going to run summer schools in the town and in Durham. At the end I felt like a pawn in a political game. I have coached at every level of the game I love, the game is close to my heart, but there weren't many happy times at Scarborough.

☐ St Jean de Luz is near Biarritz - that's going down towards the Basque country. We were on a tour there during my first year as chairman. It was my first trip abroad as a representative of the Rugby League. At the training session before the match the others tried to set me up. David Oxley came up to me and said, 'You know we've some traditions to uphold here, Bob.' I was as green as grass and eager to please. I nodded. David continued, 'Well, when you go out for the presentation they'd like you to wear a beret. You'll have noticed they all wear berets round here.' I nodded again.

'Oh, and when you shake hands, they shake with the left hand here.'

That had me a bit worried, but I thought, 'Well if that's what they do.'

Before the game started I stood in front of the mirror in the visitors' dressing room trying on this big floppy red beret. I thought it was a funny colour but David Howes reassured me.

'They wear black ones and guests wear red,' he said.

Just as I was about ready to go out on the field David Oxley came back in, took one look at me, dived into a lavatory and cracked out laughing. Only then did the penny drop.

☐ We were at an international board meeting in London and David Oxley and I were approached by a Romanian sports writer. We invited him up to my suite at the Royal Garden Hotel. He told us he had spent some time in Russia and he thought that the Soviet Union were ready to start playing Rugby League. We were naturally a bit cynical at first.

'Why are you telling us this?' we asked. 'Surely they're already established playing Rugby Union?'

He told us that things were changing in the Soviet Union. They wanted to be professional.

Myself, David Oxley and Rodney Walker went to Moscow and met with a man called Tatourian, a former international Rugby Coach. Four months previously we had sent over a package containing video footage of the game and rules translated and printed up into Russian. In that four months, Tatourian had organised a Rugby League competition with teams from as far apart as Moscow, St Petersburg and Kazakhstan, all sponsored to boot! He'd also solicited the help of a lot of former Rugby Union stars. We were impressed by the size, tenacity and pace of the Russian players and saw great potential. We agreed to employ Tatourian for two years to develop the game in Russia.

While I was in Moscow I noticed a guy sitting with a beautiful woman interpreter. It so happened that he was from Kazakhstan and had been a top Rugby Union player, coach and referee. He was called Stanislav Knorr. After the meeting he went back to Kazakhstan and within six months he had a Rugby League business going with six workers, juniors playing, the lot!

☐ We agreed to take York and Fulham to play games in Moscow, St Petersburg and Kazakhstan. Me, Mal Reilly and Phil Larder went as advance party; Phil and Mal to do the coaching and me to do the politicking, talking to government ministers, sponsors and so on.

They're great ones for statues in the Soviet Union and one day when we were in Kazakhstan they took me to see a statue of Dzahambul, the famous poet, in his home region. They put me in a car and drove me hundreds of miles. I had tea with a mayor in a village, then I went to a museum and every now and again we'd stop by the side of a road in the middle of nowhere and people would come out to meet 'the little fat bloke from England.' We'd shake hands with people and say nice things to one another and off we'd go. They took me to a state farm and sat me on a stool and paraded racehorses in front of me. I felt like the king for a day.

Next they took me to the top of a mountain with views of the deserts as far as your eyes could see. They had built a house out of sheep skins and we were to have a banquet. They'd even towed a water tank up the mountain so that I could have a wash at a sink before we started. I sat at the head of a table with my interpreter. It was covered with food. Dairy foods, salads, caviar, all set out. They handed me a bowl of sour mare's milk; I thought, 'I've got to be polite,' so I gulped it down in one. They saw me do it, thought I must like it and filled my bloody bowl up again.

They fetched a sheep's head and put it in front of me. I said to the interpreter, 'I don't think I can eat all that.' She informed me that it was part of a ritual. I had to give one of the eyes to the politician who had come with me and the other to my host. Then I had to cut a bit off for myself with a knife. They took the eyes, chewed them and spat the pupil out. I cut off a bit of cheek and ate that and then I cut a bit of neck off for the bloke who was looking after me. They told me they'd been saving their best food for over a month for me. There must have been thirty people sat at the table and they were all leaning up saying, 'Have a bit of this, try a bit of that.'

Just when I thought I was full they brought the blooming main course, lamb stew, and they were slopping it onto the plates with their hands. While all the eating was happening they were jumping up every five minutes and toasting me saying nice things and drinking vodka. Everybody has to stop when they jump up. The food goes cold with all the toasting.

Some time later when Stanislav Knorr and Nikolai Nikolaievich came to visit the English Rugby League I looked after them. One night I took them to Mamma Mia's Italian restaurant in Pontefract and they even started with the vodka toasting in there. I had to explain to the manager that's what they did in Kazakhstan.

After my banquet I had to leave the tent. They didn't have a lavatory so they told me to go down the mountain a bit. When I got back, the people I'd been eating with were all going home and then I saw some more coming. The interpreter told me that it was the second sitting. I had to go through the whole thing again. I picked and picked because I didn't want to insult them, but for two days after I didn't eat a thing.

Ne'er the twain would meet
Tradition versus new ideas

☐ A good coach learns all the time and from everybody. You can be stood at a match and overhear a five year old saying, 'Look at him, he's lazy,' and you notice that one of their forwards is hanging off the game.

I've learned a lot from these Aussie coaches. When you go into the changing room and you hear somebody with a local accent talking tactics, it goes in one ear and out of the other. When you hear the Aussie twang floating in the air it makes you listen.

☐ As coach of Great Britain I insist on preparation. If you want success you're not going to stumble over it. When Bob Beaman made his famous world record long jump in the Mexico Olympics in 1968, it didn't just happen. It wasn't a leap in the dark: he had prepared for it.

Preparation is a challenge players have to face. They are in charge of their own destiny and if they cheat, the only cheat themselves.

☐ I guess the philosophy behind playing to a system is to get all your players to a line. That doesn't mean a hierarchical line, but a line of compatibility because it is a thin line between a structure and mobility within that structure.

The old school will say, and I know this from time I spent at Barrow, that fitness, running and passing are the only important things. Not true.

What we have done in Australia is to study the game and its permutations, break it down into units and reassemble it. Once you can do that you have your blueprint - you might call it a game plan. Take for an example a tackle. If your system says that in every tackle one tackler will go low, one will go high and you will leave your opponent on his back, then when you get up you will have the leg tackler up first while the one upstairs holds the opponent down. You drill this into the players to make sure that happens. It's got to be far more effective than allowing men to run about like headless chickens. When the players understand what each other's specific job is then you start winning. The back-up to the system is statistics and data. These old coaches who won't use tackle counts and analysis of performance might as well put their heads in the sand.

There are two down sides to the system. One is that there are people who are uncoachable within it. You can get a guy who will put his heart on the line for you, who will put blood on the park, but he just can't understand a system of playing. Secondly the system can become too familiar - same club, same people, same problems, a victim of its own consistency.

☐ I don't like this new Aussie coaching system. It seems sterile. When I see wingers coming into the line, I shake my head at it.

☐ I can see the great Jim Brough now in his cap and overcoat. We had stopped at Ilkley overnight when we were down for a game with Huddersfield. We had a run round Ilkley and when we got back to our room the bulb had gone. We were feeling round for our bed when somebody put a new bulb in. Our bed was on top of the wardrobe and Jim, the old bugger, said, 'If you play as high tomorrow as you're going to sleep tonight, you've no trouble.'

☐ There are two problems we need to face when introducing Rugby League and university graduates to one another. For a start, Rugby League clubs don't seem to understand that academics want to study as well as play. They need to understand that to a lot of lads studying comes first. I know of a lad at Chester College who has been told 'Either you come to play for us or you get kicked into touch.'

The second point is the Rugby League establishment itself. They say that for pragmatic reasons they want graduates to play the game, because when these sort of people get into powerful positions they will promote the game. I'm glad they made that statement because there are quality people who are in love with Rugby League. But I'm afraid we will lose students if opportunities for employment in administrative positions don't arise. We don't want graduates volunteering to coach Oulton under 11s. They need positions of responsibility, particularly if they've got degrees in Sports Administration, Marketing or Business Studies. There are students now who are ready to test the water and they will want to have their say. They are intelligent enough to realise that it can't always happen their way although sometimes the way students act you'd think they had no bloody brains at all, but they do have the ability to think and rationalise.

☐ Five or six years ago the budget for student Rugby was about £10,000. Last year the budget for the domestic programme was £60,000 and the international scene has really mushroomed. The Student World Cup alone had a budget of £130,000. We have an office at Rugby League HQ and one at Oxford University. We hold an annual Varsity match between Oxford and Cambridge. Imagine that a few years ago!

☐ In the past we were called UCARLA and we were under the umbrella of the British Amateur Rugby League. Now we are Student Rugby because it's not just universities. The policy years ago was to forget Rugby Union people and concentrate on the lads who had never played Rugby before. This meant you got lads who had nothing better to do and the standard was rubbish. No quality, no organisation. This was the problem with Rugby League in development areas. Now we try to introduce Union lads to the game. You can't just pick up a Union lad and carry him to League, but we can coax them.

☐ One thing I've noticed creeping into student Rugby League is verbal abuse. This has been almost a ritual in traditional amateur Rugby League for a long time. Now as more working class Northern lads have started going to college they have brought some of their tricks with them.

I was at a League match at Nottingham Polytechnic which is almost exclusively Rugby Union. They were playing Leeds Poly, who are probably the best student team. I heard the Leeds full back give his first tactical talk. 'Right

lads, let's knock their fucking heads off.' At half-time I reminded Charlie Tidball, the referee, that we were clamping down on verbal abuse and after the game I told the players not to do it in future. The Leeds stand-off half, a real dyed-in-the-wool Rugby League lad, was not happy. He said that it was acceptable psychological warfare. I explained to him that it wasn't in student Rugby League. My argument was that this is the hardest of physical games to start with and that if you're talking you're not acting. He seemed to understand in the end.

☐ At one time you played either Rugby Union or Rugby League and ne'er the twain would meet. The attitude we want to breed amongst university lads is that they have their own chance to decide their preference. Now a lot of universities have combined Rugby Union and League clubs and they play on the same field, which would have been unheard of in the past. This sometimes means that the Rugby League lads have to play on a field with Union markings, but if you've got a co-operative groundsman like the one at Crewe and Alsager College, you can get him to put in the extra time to mark the field.

☐ Most people who go to university are from the higher social classes. In these classes Rugby Union is 'The Game.' This leaves us with a mountain to climb. We don't want to set up in opposition, but we need to get footholds.

☐ My faith in Rugby Union is not so great. Take the star players in both codes and you will see the massive gulf between us.

Rugby Union has long regarded Rugby League has an illegitimate brother, born out of wedlock in 1895. First they denied he existed, then they tried to forget about him, locked him away in a cupboard. But he still comes back to haunt them. He haunts the well-educated, the solicitors, the insurance brokers, the doctors and the bankers. And they see that he has not only bettered himself, but he is better than them. The well-educated are crossing the line to Rugby League. The only thing I envy Rugby Union for at the moment is the quality of the administration. They envy me my players.

☐ Apart from my family, I have three threads that run through my life: politics, faith and Rugby League. I am fortunate enough to be paid to be a politician, I am honoured to be a Methodist local preacher and I live and breath Rugby League. I treat all three passions with the same intensity.

At one time in my life the Labour Party was in the doldrums, my local church had closed and Wigan had been relegated to the Second Division. Those were the dark days. Had things gone right on April 9th 1992 at the General Election then life would be near to perfection.

I know how great the game is and, just as importantly, the culture that goes with it. Just as I want to spread the word of my politics and faith, so I want others to share with me my enthusiasm for a sport that is more than a game. When I stop doing that, it will be because the culture will have changed and Rugby League will have become just another sport.

☐ In 1985 when I was elected to the European Parliament, myself and Brian Simpson, another Rugby League fanatic set up a group of MEPs to promote Rugby League. It's been a great success. Freddy Blak, a Danish MEP, is our President and what a great fan he now is. When we made him President, he knew nothing about Rugby League or Rugby in general. His commitment is such that he went to Melbourne for the second Test in 1992. His lasting memory is of his wife shouting, 'Get them on-side' in the excitement of her first ever match. She is now also a great fan.

☐ I went to a school that had a lot of Asian and West Indian kids in it. My best mate was Mohammed Butt, better known as Tony, the brother of a well-known ex-Leeds player, Ikram Butt. They had all been to the famous Rugby League playing junior school, Royal Park in Leeds. A great number of Asian lads play Rugby League at that age. It's a pity not a lot of them choose to carry on. I always think the youngest of the Butt brothers, Iman, would have made a great career. But I've heard that a lot of the mams and dads in the Asian community don't encourage their sons to make a career in the game.

☐ Modern technology has led to remarkable changes in the treatment of injuries sustained on the Rugby field. Although the types of injury sustained have changed little during my fifty years' experience, treatment has improved immeasurably and physiotherapists are now putting players back on the field in a much shorter time. Minor injuries, bumps and bruises are treated initially with ice, now readily available. Blisters, grazes and cuts present few problems, but major ones - some quite obvious like fractures and dislocations and others less obvious - can prove difficult.

The most serious fractures are those of the spine, the thigh bone, and those involving joint structures. Dislocations are most common at the shoulder and the finger joints, but can occur at the ankle, knee, elbow and even the hip.

Inflammation of bursae, the sac-like structures which lessen friction over bony protuberances, can be a nuisance but rarely keep a player from the game for very long. Strapping - a useful adjunct in the treatment of strains and sprains - is also used to enable a player to resume playing earlier by giving him confidence knowing that his injury is supported and protected. The physiotherapist plays a major role in the running of a Rugby League football club.

☐ This season the authorities have introduced the 'Blood Bin', that means that if a player is bleeding and it won't stop, you have to go off for treatment. It's a bit hard on us players, but I think it's to do with AIDS and that, so we've got to take it seriously.

I must have been one of the first players to go off for it. It was in the first ten minutes of the first game of the season. I was getting up after a tackle and this big prop forward kicked me straight in the nose. Well, it wouldn't stop bleeding. I hoped the referee wouldn't notice because I wanted to carry on but he came running straight over to me. He shouted to our physio to come on. The physio, Dave they call him, tried to stem the blood with a towel, but it still wouldn't stop so that was that. The referee pulled a card out of his top pocket, a white one with a red cross on, and off I went.

I was lucky that they stopped the blood after a few minutes and I was able to go back on, otherwise I'd have spent my first game of the season sat on the bench watching.

☐ I suppose I wanted to be like my heroes and idols, that's what sets you off playing. I started off wanting to play for Featherstone, my home town. It was to do with pride and following in the footsteps of great players I'd been brought up with. When I left Featherstone, I signed for Oldham on the Saturday afternoon and was expected to play in the first team straightaway the next day. I got up on the Sunday morning and I didn't want to go. My wife phoned up Tex Hudson and he came over and had a good talk to me. He had played for a few different clubs and he talked about the benefits. I gave in and went to Oldham but it took some doing.

☐ One thing the players contract system has done is stop under-the-counter payments to senior professionals. It has also helped some players make a full time living out of the game. In my case I had to decide which was my first choice for full time job. I was still employed at the pit. I had to decide which to devote my time to, Rugby or Coal Board. The other side of it is that a lot a mediocre players got good contracts because the employers panicked in their efforts

to obtain a binding agreement for the players. Some players who call themselves full-time Rugby League professionals aren't really. I call them unemployed rugby players, because their earning potential has actually gone down. Before the contract, system a player could easily have a full-time job as well as be paid for playing Rugby. There isn't that much you can do with rugby players for eight hours a day either. Physical training has to be limited and sitting them down to watch techniques on video soon gets boring.

If people are naive enough to believe that illegal approaches to players have stopped since the contract system has started then they're wrong, the same with tempting young players to sign. The bigger clubs, under the guise of scouting, are still taking 14 or 15 year old lads out with their mams and dads for meals.

□ In November 1990 the Queen opened the new BARLA headquarters in Huddersfield. A few days after, one of the Queen's flunkeys wrote on her behalf, 'thank you for the delicious lunch and an enjoyable day'. He ended the letter with 'A warm thanks for the balls and jerseys which I'm sure will be popular with the Queen's grandchildren.' Now can you imagine that! Can you see Wills and Harry turning out for Hull Dockers or Dewsbury Celtic.

□ Rotherham Rangers are struggling to keep the flame of Amateur Rugby League flickering in what is known as a Development Area. They enjoy their Rugby League and, because they know what it is like to struggle, always make sure that their end-of-season tour is in one of the farther flung outposts of Amateur Rugby League. They have toured Holland, Cambridge and the West Country.

On the West Country tour they played a team in Plymouth. This game recalled scenes from Roman times right up to the present day. I have many memories of the coverage of the media of the Gulf War. One of them is General 'Stormin' Norman Schwarzkopf marching in to press conferences in full desert uniform complete with sidearm flanked by hatchet-faced troops armed to the teeth with automatic weapons. Julius Caesar must have looked similar in many ways striding around Rome with his Praetorian Guard. It was down to the Rotherham Raiders to bring us right up to date, in their game against Plymouth which was held on the sports field of the local Royal Marines base.

They were accompanied step for step by a platoon of hard case Marine Commandos armed with vicious looking new SA80 automatic rifles. No words, smiles or gestures were exchanged as the grim-faced troops made sure that these possible spetznatz insurgents didn't wreak havoc upon their strategically vital rugby ground.

□ A mate of mine played for Batley in the early 80s. This was in the days when shirt sponsorship first started and sure enough The Gallant Youths had managed to get in on the act.

Their benefactor was a firm who had a branch which dealt with wholesale domestic supplies, you know the sort of thing, cleaning materials, disinfectant and Shake and Vac.

Things took an ominous tone when the new strip with corporate logo on the chest arrived. For a start Bukta had got the colours wrong and the lads found themselves wearing pink and orange hoops. Henry Oulton the Youths' big-kicking fullback, whose best days had been spent at Wakefield Trinity, was determinedly trying to peel the lettering from the front of his jumper. His philosophy was, being a pro, that if he wasn't getting paid for wearing writing on his chest then it was coming off.

The next bad omen was the appearance in the dressing room of the Managing Director of the firm. Although he never described his appearance to me, I sense a smell of cheap cigars and Brut in the room whenever he told me this story. I found myself seeing sovereign rings, camel-hair coats and white slip-on moccasins in my mind's eye whenever I thought about his appearance in the Batley dressing room that day.

He'd decided that what was lacking at Mount Pleasant on match days was a bit of razzmatazz. If you've been to Mount Pleasant you'll know that what is really lacking is shelter from the wind that comes smacking down the Pennines. Nevertheless he'd seen videos of some of the big Australian games no doubt, and decided that this was the way forward. The adolescent girls of the Heavy Wollen district have every reason to be grateful that he didn't decide to recruit cheerleaders that year, because hypothermia can be very unpleasant.

The boss of Batley's new sponsors had decided to promote their products by chucking a few freebies from the cheaper end of the product range into the crowd. Here things stopped becoming ominous, they became doom laden. Doom laden because the cardboard boxes of gifts for the long suffering Batley faithful were full of toilet rolls and light bulbs.

It could still have turned out all right if Batley had won. Unfortunately, their playing record in those days gave no cause for optimism.

The points against Batley started to build up, slowly at first, but nothing that their supporters weren't used to. In the second half the lads began to tire and a rout was on the cards.

The Batley fans reacted in a way which is as old as spectator sport itself, a direct descendant of the thumbs down given by Caesar to vanquished gladiators with a nod in the direction of the British archers who gave their defeated enemies the two fingers at Agincourt.

First an isolated bog roll, followed by the odd 60 watt carton, crossed over onto the pitch from the sparsely populated terracing.

Then, once everybody realised that it was okay to do it, a bombardment of cheap domestic goods littered the in-goal area where the Batley players were spending much of their time.

They won't go for razzmatazz at Batley any more. The team are now sponsored by Fox's Biscuits and a full tin is what you get for a winning bonus.

□ At one time the local printer used to print posters about three foot long by two foot wide that were pasted up on street corners every other week. They used to tell you who the local team were playing and the kick off time. Those, along with the odd hand-written newspaper placard that said things like 'latest county selections', were the only visual signs of Rugby being played in the district. In the last few years, Stones Bitter, Silk Cut and Sky Television have all bought space on those big More O'Ferrel hoardings to promote the game. The last I've

seen recently was one for Nike trainers with a ten foot high image of Martin Offiah streaking away with the ball underneath the words 'Your hands can't catch what your eyes can't see.'

Nothing in the world quite like it
The international arena

□ It was a summer evening and my mum had dropped us off at Leeds. We had come to watch Leeds's second team play Moscow Magicians. It was the first time I had ever seen or heard of a Russian team. I was so excited, I couldn't wait to sit down. I'd heard Ikram Butt played for Leeds. There was a bunch of Leeds United fans beside us. They shouted very loud like most fans. Moscow played quite well at first, but because they weren't used to it they got tired. I think the final score was 36 - 16 to Leeds, but Moscow were good.

□ The two most common misconceptions about Rugby League in Australia are that it is played in constant sunshine and on pleasant, modern grounds. I was cured of both of these false impressions by Henson Park.

The 1981 season in Sydney was remarkable for a couple of things. It was the year that Parramatta (with Kenny, Stirling, Ella,

Cronin, Grothe and co) won their first Premiership, but far more surprising than that was that their nearest challengers, and the team they eventually beat in the Grand Final, were Newtown. Newtown were a declining inner city club who, within a couple of years, would be kicked out of the competition altogether. But in 1981 with John Ferguson, among others, in their side, they had a memorable swansong.

Newtown were quite often selected for the televised Saturday match. That meant that I spent what seemed like an eternity of Saturdays at Henson Park, a crumbling old ground with a stand that held about one bus load. It was always raining and the press box was always full to overflowing, so there was little alternative but to stand on the hill and get soaked. One afternoon was worse than all the others; the rain was coming down by the bathfull and the grass underfoot had achieved the liquid texture of a 70s rock festival. In search of whatever shelter there might be, a handful of us were huddling by the fence that separated the ground from the back gardens of the adjoining houses. It was something else that was typical of Newtown, that people used to watch from those gardens, climbing up step ladders so that they could see. I wasn't surprised, therefore, when a voice from above said: 'Jeez mate, you'se getting pissed wet through down there.'

I'd visions of a spare umbrella or a sou'wester, but when he came back it was to pass me a length of old lino. I was grateful enough to have it and it did the job after a fashion. But as I stood there clutching a lump of lino above my head, watching Henson Park dissolve around me and peering through the waterfall to see whether the ball was going anywhere near Chicka Ferguson, I couldn't help reflecting: 'this was what the Australian game was all about.'

☐ Whenever I've been on tour I've always told the Great Britain players not to grab for their food and try to be well mannered. That's what I call social organisation. It is sensible and managerial. When my players are interviewed they come over articulate and well mannered. I think when the television did the documentary about Orrell Rugby Union and Wigan Rugby League they expected the Rugby League lads to be uncouth and loutish. They wanted to see foul mouths, blood and guts, but they got neat suits and ties. On the field some of our lads can assassinate with the best, but off the field they can also be dignified and gentle.

☐ There is nothing in the world of Rugby League that quite prepares you for Papua New Guinea. There are people in Wigan and Featherstone who are fanatical about the game, but nothing like the depth of feeling that there is in PNG, where, for a lot of people, it is all they have. It is also the one real unifying factor in a country where there are hundreds of different languages and where the older people in some tribes grew up believing sincerely that they were the only people on the planet.

Everyone in the country seems to follow the game, in their own country and overseas, with a religious devotion. Small wonder that the sight of British or Australian players playing, training, or just arriving at an airport causes such a stir.

None of us in 1990 was sure a couple of days before we were due to set off that we were going to be able to get into the country. The PNG government was particularly jumpy about journalists and it took an age for the visas to come through.

Even when we landed in the vicious heat of Port Moresby, it seemed that there were still problems. A very official-looking official took what seemed like an hour examining every page of my passport and cross checking with various other documents. Finally, he gave me a stern glance and told me ,'I cannot let you into Papua New Guinea...'

Terrific, I thought, twenty hours in the air, a couple of thousand quid and I'm not even going to get out of the airport. But he carried on, 'I cannot let you into Papua New Guinea,' he said, 'until you answer for me one question. Why does Ellery Hanley not come with you?'

☐ On one of the tours to New Zealand, Great Britain were due to play a game at Whangerei. We set off from Auckland but had only got about half way when our car broke down. A bus load of supporters from Auckland pulled up nearby for a mass relief stop. I managed to wangle a lift with them while my cousin said he would stop with the car which was going to take about three hours to mend. He would see me after the game.

When I got on the bus and we set off it was obvious that alcohol had been flowing for some time. A rather large Maori came up to me, surveyed my GB shirt and said, 'Hey mate, my ancestors used to eat yours!'

This was just the kind of thing I wanted to hear, thirteen thousand miles from home and surrounded by people I didn't know. Of course, the tension relaxed once I had paid my way into the beer fund and opened a bottle of Steinlager.

☐ Prince's Park, Second Test, thirty-one thousand on a Friday night and out come the teams at last to the strains of *Land of Hope and Glory*. We all gave vent: 'We hate Papua New Guinea/We hate New Zealand too/We hate France and Australia/But Britain we love you'. Next, *God Save the Queen* filled the Melbourne night. Impressive, nay inspirational stuff, this. Proud, heady moments for an exiled Pom. The reality, as it is wont to do, crept in. The rain began to pour and God, but those Aussies looked damned huge. Maybe the good and warm feeling I'd had about tonight was more to do with sentiment and my wife's dinner than the chance of a happy ending.

But not so. Reilly's boys were indeed to make this a memorable night to be British. They were truly superb. This wasn't just a win, this was a massacre. Images I hope to recall at the end of my days abounded. Such as Shaun Edwards tackling the mighty Harragon head-on at the height of the second half Aussie storm; Garry Schofield calming and positioning an excited Martin Offiah before handing him the perfect pass for the inevitable icing-on-the-cake try; and finally ex-Northerner Kelvin Skerrett, dragging his wearied body from the field after giving his heroic all. This was the stuff of epic poems. Like beating Halifax and Leeds in the same week. Well, nearly as good anyway.

And then there was the crowd. And what a crowd. I'd forgotten just how magnificent a British crowd in full voice can be, *Here We Go* and *I'd Rather Be a Pom Than a Con* stunning the Melbornians. They'd never seen the like. That massive, awe-inspiring, *You'll Never Walk Alone* near the end brought tears to many an eye. The over-riding memory, the one that will vividly remain as others begin to fade, 29 - 10 with just a few minutes to go. The game was well and truly won. I looked behind me to the British fans and what a sight I saw! There were about seven thousand people dancing in the aisles, on the seats, even on the fence and all as one singing, *Always Look on the Bright Side of Life*. The party was in full swing.

As for those Aussies around me, well, in what is mostly the typical Australian way they took it on the chin, shook my hand and we wished each other well. After all, there's always the next time and seven thousand Poms can't all be wrong - always look on the bright side of life.

☐ I've now become a Great Britain Rugby League supporter - you don't see many games but certainly travel further. I decided this after joining Peter Banner's Club-Strength World Tour to Australia last year.

Our party stopped off at New York, San Francisco and Honolulu. This took two weeks so by the time we arrived on Aussie soil most of us had to be reminded that we had gone for the Rugby! Adjusting from being a holidaymaker to a Rugby League supporter took time but after

donning our British shell suits we set off for the first match we were to take in at Parramatta. Signed in at their social club we were guided into the carvery and treated to their four dollar roast - how do they do it? They put our club facilities to shame.

By the time we arrived at the Gold Coast game the travelling army of Great Britain fans had increased to nearly ten thousand. Imagine my surprise when the Coach, Mal Reilly, approached me in the club after the game and asked me whether I'd seen Phil Lowe. We saw many celebrities on our travels including Ellery Hanley. He brushed past our party after the game showing an incredible side-step, hailed a taxi and sped off into the night. Wonderful public relations from our skipper.

Lang Park was slightly intimidating. Walking the mile or so from the town centre to the stadium the locals were friendly enough, but after the skinful of Powers and Toohey's before and during the match, their mood changed dramatically. Free buses back to town were announced over the loud speakers. But where did they depart from? Only the locals knew and they weren't telling us. As the loaded buses sped past us, hostile banter and abuse came through their open windows, leaving us Poms to retrace our footsteps back to the safety of our hotel rooms.

Camcorders were in abundance. Mine never left my neck to record faithfully the trip of a lifetime. Five and three quarter hours of video to be precise!

Memories of the tour are numerous, some daunting such as the Blue Mountains Skyway and the Scenic Railway ride. Death defying, white knuckle rides indeed, and we were nowhere near a theme park! On the whole though most memories were very pleasant indeed. I can't wait for 1996 when we're off again, with a bit of luck!

The passion of northern culture
Media and sponsorship

☐ I think we're lucky in being a parochial sport, to get the amount of sponsorship we get. A lot of people talk about the hypocrisy involved in advertising tobacco through sport but the hypocrisy goes deeper than that. Me and David Oxley went to the Euro Parliamentary Group in Strasbourg. Two out of the fifteen who turned up smoked. The guy who said, 'Tobacco advertising will be banned' was chain smoking. The EEC spends millions of pounds developing the third world tobacco industry and allows Greece, one of its members, to export tobacco to the third world.

I didn't realise how clever tobacco advertising was. If you get to twenty-one without smoking you are unlikely to start. And people who stop are replaced by children who take it up. I don't like it, but without tobacco and beer sponsorship, what do we do?

☐ When we go to the Silk Cut Draw we get cigarettes given and sometimes the odd biro or lighter. It's become a ritual that you go for breakfast on the morning of the first round draw. If I get as much as two rashers and a link of sausage, that's as much as I get out of it. When BSB first started up they offered the board of directors a saucer apiece but we turned them down.

☐ At Sky Eddie and me try to present the game as it is, not as we think it should be presented. We have no qualms about pointing out mistakes but we try to make it interesting. You can't change a bad game into a good one, no-one gets a nail biter every week. If no tries are scored we talk about the defences being on top. If you don't have the hype, you don't have the fans. We look upon ourselves as explainers as well as commentators. When somebody scores a try and the screens show a close-up of a man with a smiling face, we like to tell the viewers that it was his fifteenth try this season.

☐ You spread the gospel by being 'popular'. Sky Sports uses gimmicks in order to attract new people, non-Rugby League people you might call them. The Head of Sport here is the man who introduced night-time cricket and Daffy Duck walking across the screen to Australia.

☐ I genuinely hope that Sky Television can bring the passion of northern culture to the television screens. We could make Rugby League popular in the South, as it ought to be. I won't knock the BBC for their past coverage of the game, but we're the new kids on the TV block and we can breathe a breath of fresh air into the coverage of the game. For a start, I'd like to see the ref miked. How often does a man on the terraces question why a ref has given a particular decision? It would be nice to hear the explanation.

TV often gets accused of messing about with games, but so does every entrepreneur. I don't see that it makes much difference if we hold up a game for a minute because of adverts. If we're helping to popularise the sport then the knock-on effect is good for all concerned. Times are changing. Rugby League players are PR conscious; they're bursting out of the northern enclave. They're realising that the wider world is interested in them. I was at the crowning of Lennox Lewis and I saw Martin Offiah there.

☐ I know that there is an attitude amongst some older players who think that modern players are overpaid, that they are soft buggers and that Rugby League doesn't owe anybody a living. These are usually the ones who missed out on the big money. It is patently obvious to us working in the media that the players now are faster, fitter, better defensively, better able to score tries and, whether we like it or not, more open to Australian systems of play. Let's face it, if something is successful, we'd be stupid not to follow it.

☐ I like to interview Gary Jack, Sheffield's Australian full back. He should be on a stage not a rugby field, he has such a dry sense of humour. After the game Eagles played against Australia I was in the dressing room with him and he was looking a bit downhearted.

'It must be difficult playing against your own country,' I ventured.

'Yes, yes,' he said, getting his kit together. I tried a different tack.

'You're playing against Wakefield Trinity on Sunday, Gary. How are you going to tackle them?'

There was a long pause. I watched him, you could almost see the cogs turning in his mind. Then in his strong Aussie accent he said, 'Round the legs, I guess, Claire.'

☐ TV is a privileged spectator to this great game. When we commentate we go for accuracy, we emphasise the athletic, we present the emotion, the tension and draw from what goes on on the field. It is a labour of love. We never sit on a wide shot. The main philosophy is to keep the action going on the screen. We emphasise the big hits, the kicks to the line and concentrate on the positives. We're a communications network trying to sell a product. We've got the fastest production crew in television. Within three seconds we can have a replay of any action and a name caption on the screen. We do occasionally get accused of showing just the big games but the programme is called *The Big League* and if you take the cream the rest comes to the top. Judging by the response we get to *Boots and All*, letters from as far afield as Cambridge and Renfrew, Scotland, the word is spreading.

☐ The Aussies have been quick off the mark to notice the more sophisticated side to the game's image. They like all the hype, glamour and razzmatazz. When you get top singers like Tina Turner slithering down players' legs on the video, all sexy and stripped off, it means they're looking beyond the gas tanks and industry and all the other images that you normally associate with this game.

☐ The first time I ever entered a dressing room to do interviews I was really thrown in at the deep end. I wanted to see behind the scenes of a radio station as part of my college work. I went in one day to Hallam FM; the Sports Editor was opening a letter. He looked up and said, 'Right Claire. Get a UHER.' (That's a tape machine.) 'Get over to Don Valley. There's some important news about the Eagles and I want you to do some interviewing.'

I had never done anything like that before. I had flu and I was supposed to go up to people I'd idolised on telly and interview them. By the time I got there I was shaking. Whitbread had extended their sponsorship deal with the Eagles so I interviewed their rep, Gary Hethrington, Mark Aston and Darryl Powell. I told them all I'd never done anything like this before. They all knew but they treated me with good manners.

☐ I have made a New Year resolution that I am not going to buy the *League Express*, the *Rugby Leaguer* and *Open Rugby*. I am not going to watch *Boots and All* and I'm definitely going to switch the local radio stations off. They are anti-establishment, hostile to the game and by implication they say that the Rugby League doesn't know what it is doing. People ringing in for catch questions, teasers and bloody trivia. And it's often factually incorrect. I can remember talking to Bill Broxup, the Chairman at Castleford, in 1969. He said, 'Harry, the wireless wants to come, but they don't want to bloody pay us. They're going to take the bloody fans off us if we're not careful.'

I think I know about Rugby League enough to say we shouldn't be used by the media and the trivial media at that. It's coming to a crunch where great decisions are going to have to be made.

☐ I am disappointed with social, you might call them class, attitudes in this country. England is not the centre of the world, English attitudes are not always right. We have a lot to learn. In the Maori culture of New Zealand and, to generalise, the Polynesian cultures, they have a far more relaxed attitude. They're bonded by strong family values, they know when to cuddle their youngsters and they hold their older people in awe. People are not judged by the way they speak or the side of town they come from.

In some respects that's why Sky Television has been good for Rugby League. They're using Australian methods, an Aussie is an Aussie, you see. They don't have the hang-ups about class and the history. They bring a much needed freshness. They promote the athletic content, they say what an excellent athlete Garry Schofield is rather than a man who speaks with an accent. It upsets me, even angers me, when I see it done the other way round.

Making people sit back and think
The new administrators

☐ I started as a secretary at the Headquarters and now I'm Head of Player Personnel. That means I deal with discipline, drug taking, contracts, clearances to play, transfers and work permits. It doesn't feel like a particularly sexist game to work in, although I understand that the wives of people like committee men at the clubs have a harder time. They are the unpaid labour like the wives at golf and cricket clubs. I remember the first time I ever used my official Rugby League pass to get into a game. It was at Wakefield Trinity and the gateman said, 'Whose wife are you then, love?' This was in 1983. I was flabbergasted, but I just left it at that.

☐ I was a cleaner here for two years before the new regime came in. Now I do a bit of catering. Since Maurice Lindsay came we've moved away from cold buffets and on to cooked lunches. When the BBC came we had fillet steak. When it's just an ordinary board meeting we have cottage pie or maybe soup to start. It's smashing here, we're all on first name terms. And I love

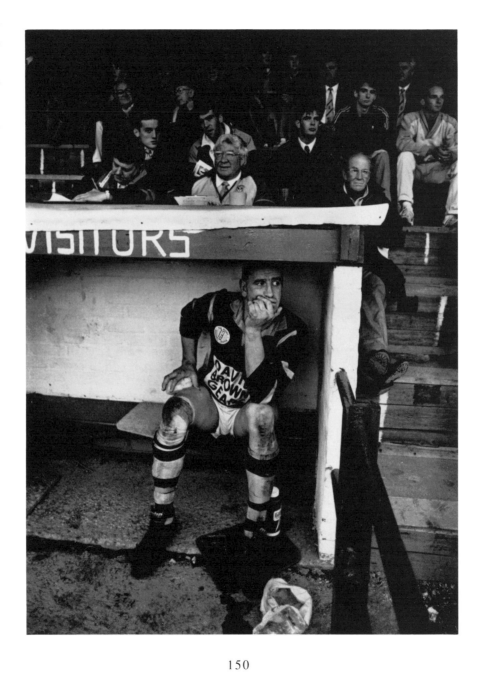

150

Bob Ashby's laugh, I don't know what they do in them board meetings, but you can hear Bob's laugh above them all.

☐ I was the first woman to get an interview for a Rugby League Development Officer's post. It was for Oldham District. They said to me on the phone that if Neil Woods hadn't got it, I would have. It must have made a few people sit back and think about women coming to this level.

☐ While I think women should enjoy it, men should play it. I'd rather watch a bloke play than a woman and not just to admire their bodies. The only time I hate being at a rugby ground is when the men start coming out with the same old bullshit. 'Go home and get the puddings in,' or 'Go home to the dishes,' we've heard it so many times.

☐ A lot of sexism exists at board level with some of the, shall we say, more traditional clubs. I was a director at Carlisle until last year and as a woman I found myself barred from several boardrooms. The first time it happened I had blithely followed my colleagues into the room before being politely asked to leave. I thought it was an April Fool's Day joke.

At Barrow I complained bitterly about my treatment and the *Barrow Evening Mail*

highlighted my attempts to gain entry to the boardroom as 'the best try at Craven Park this season'.

☐ Batley were playing well that year. The young side led by George Pieniazek, a young, innovative and enthusiastic coach, were top of the Second Division. After Christmas was out of the way it was time to start dreaming about Wembley and the Challenge Cup.

The Gallant Youths were drawn away to Wigan. The team were excited rather than daunted. They believed that they could cause a sensation rather than take a beating and a pay day like a punch drunk sparring partner.

In the week preceding the match Wigan were to play a re-arranged League fixture at Central Park. Their opponents were Widnes who in those days were in their pomp. The hope was that Widnes would do Batley a favour by sapping the strength of the Wigan players and, to be brutally honest, injuring a few.

The Batley Chairman spoke to George about the cup tie.

'I'll do anything I can to help you prepare the side for the game,' he said.

'Well how about getting to the Wigan-Widnes game on Wednesday night?'

'Fine,' said the Chairman.

'Can our kid come as well?'

'Er ... OK,' said the Chairman.

'What about our lass?'

'Go on then,' said the Chairman.

They set off to Central Park in the Chairman's white XJS. When they arrived all the Chairman had to say was, 'We're the party from Batley,' and all doors opened. You could call it style, but you would be meaning brass neck.

After the game the 'we're the party from Batley' technique found the little group in the Wigan boardroom drinking tea from china cups. Everybody in the room was being extra polite to the little Batley group, especially to George's wife. George also noticed that every now and then people were giving them strange looks which he put down to the fact that they were hicks from the Heavy Woollen district.

As everyone was preparing to leave, the Wigan Chairman approached George Pieniazek's wife and started to make polite but strained small talk, then he said, 'Do you realise that in the eighty-odd years that this boardroom has existed, other than the cleaner you are the first woman to have set foot in it,' and, extra politely, bid them all good night.

☐ When BARLA first started we'd be up while three in the morning answering letters and put the kids to bed at various stages. We prided ourselves at the time that for every letter

Fallowfield put out attacking us, we had one back within twenty-four hours. Ann, our eleven year old, would be collating; Richard, he was six, would be folding and putting into envelopes, and as soon as Gerard got to two we had him licking the envelopes. Some mornings we went to work with 300 letters to post. When I used to get to work late the boss would look at me and say, 'One of these days, Keaveney, you're going to run out of excuses.' I even used the YEB's number where I worked as a contact number in the BARLA handbook.

All the hard work became worthwhile when the Sports Council described amateur Rugby League as the most progressive sport in the country.

☐ I saw David Oxley quoted in the *Daily Mirror* as saying 'When we set up BARLA' meaning they had been involved. I thought, 'Who's all this we?' I couldn't recall him being at the Greenside Working Men's Club for the first meeting and stuffing envelopes half the night. I wrote to the *Daily Mirror* Mailbag. When I saw David Oxley he smiled and apologised and said it was a slip of the tongue.

☐ I came to Rugby League HQ as a professional, an accountant. My contact with Rugby League had been because my family came from Warrington. I have to admit I preferred soccer and spent twenty five-years on the terraces at Gigg Lane watching Bury. I think you need to be an aficionado to watch Rugby League.

When I first came here I was surprised to find that in a professional sport so many clubs were run on a part-time basis. In recent years a lot of money has been spent in the game by otherwise level-headed businessmen, splashing out to achieve winners. A lot of people are going to have to realise that the value for money comes from what is put in.

As an administrator I suppose I ought to be impartial but if I haven't been to a game at the weekend, when I look in the paper I always look for Warrington's results first. You build up loyal ties to family which are difficult to alter. My family are from Warrington and you know what they say about where the heart is.

☐ When I was co-opted onto the Board I was given the job of raising money through sponsorship. Up to that day I had never sold anything bar myself. I spoke through my hands as a builder. Now I get a big kick out of seeing people have a civilised day out in a box at a Rugby League match. In this game we can tailor the corporate hospitality to suit the family image, and the ones who taste it along with the sandwiches we provide are pleasantly surprised. When they can look round and say, 'Ooh, so and so's here!' that's great. I can't stress the family image enough. We have a good product to sell to the public. When you travel to away games to places like Carlisle and people are setting up a picnic on the way you know it's good. And so do firms like Barclays Bank.

☐ When we challenged the old Board about its stewardship one of the lads said, 'I know why you are here and what question you're going to ask.' They knew because I'd been asking the same question for four years:

'Why was it when BNF sponsored us to the tune of £60,000 they've spent it on one player, Rob Ackerman, rather than spread it around buying the players we really need?'

I knew the answer. What was at stake was three years' guaranteed sponsorship with one year's guarantee on top. The sponsor gave the money so the sponsor picked the man. It wasn't necessarily the best way to have used that sort of money.

☐ Being on a Rugby League Club committee is like being a social worker. I'm a school governor for the same reason. My wife plays pop with me because I'm thinking and living it all the time.

I did the accounts for Castleford in 1948 and the committee then was a typical small town set up. Gideon Shaw was a local printer so he did the printing. There was a man they called 'Chocolate Box' Walter Smith who had a shop, Harry Robshaw, a builder, and Stanley Hirst, a butcher who provided the pork pies. Now you've got people in the game with yachts moored up at Hull. But most of all, it's the players themselves who are the nouveau riche of Rugby League.

Class War
Clearing away old regimes

☐ It was getting dark as we drove through the outer suburbs of Leeds on the way home from a match. The kids were a bit restless in the back of the car. They were tired after the excitement and were struggling to get comfortable and falling out with each other a bit as each encroached on the other's space.

There wasn't much traffic on this bleak stretch of dual carriageway flanked by dog-eared tower blocks and derelict garment factories. We came to some traffic lights and pulled alongside an immaculate black, top of the range Mitsubishi four wheel drive with tinted windows and thick, wide tyres. It also had one of those personalised numberplates, part of which consisted of the letters ELL.

The kids were distracted from their tired fractiousness by their curiosity about this extremely street-credible set of wheels. There was a black guy in a baseball hat at the wheel. Eye to eye contact between him and the small occupants on the back seat brought squeals of recognition.

'It's Ellery Hanley! Let's burn him off!'

After some mutual face pulling, a very good attempt at portraying abject fear by Great Britain's supposedly humourless and unapproachable skipper showed that he accepted the challenge from our rather beat up Ford, but knew he had no chance.

The lights turned green. Ellery crawled away from the junction looking as though he was trying to squeeze every ounce of power from his engine. We chugged away from him in triumph, the kids cheering and waving as we left him behind. I looked round. Ellery had a grin on his face which only diminished in size in relation to the distance which grew between us and him. The kids forgot that they were tired and that their elbows were sticking into each other and I remembered that you should take people as you find them, or at least try now and again.

☐ When our Craig, that's my youngest, talks about Rugby League, he says, 'She plays,' and when he talks about players, he says, 'Brenda and Geraldine' and so on. Instinctively we sometimes say, 'Mark your man' or something, but once at a presentation they said, 'Man of the Match award' and it didn't half stick out to the two teams of women.

☐ Rugby players had seriously bad haircuts in the 1970s. Feather cuts, side burns, the lot. And the clothes! Say no more! High waist bands, loons, jumpers with three stars on and yellow shirts with huge winged collars. Mind you, I was as bad, I remember going to watch Widnes at Odsal in the semi-final of the Challenge Cup. It was the time when Red Rum was winning the Grand National every year and T. Rex and Slade were always at number one. I strode up the hill in a pair of bright orange platform shoes with four inch heels, Oxford bags that were the greenest bright green you've ever seen and a hair cut like David Bowie on the *Aladdin Sane* cover.

☐ There is a certain young Rovers player who spent a miserable two weeks in Benidorm with the monk on. In the night clubs around where he lived the girls adored him and he always had a gang of them round him. In Benidorm it didn't happen and he found it hard to understand why.

☐ The Wakefield Panthers always go to away matches in track suits. Everybody comments that

we're a smart team, I can't believe how professional we are. A bloke from Halifax called Ernest always comes up to us and says, 'You're superstars.' Everybody talks about us, we are the Wigan of women's Rugby League.

☐ When I moved to Hull, Arthur Bunting told me that as soon as he had persuaded Vince Farrar to sign he would be able to rebuild the team around West Riding forwards. The people in Hull treated us like idols. They would be queuing up in the car park to get our autographs. Many a time these days I go back to my scrapbook and have a look. And I still get recognised. I was on my holidays in Blackpool and a Widnes supporter came up.

He said, 'Will you sit my little lad on your knee while I take a photo?'

It's nice when that happens.

☐ After our Paul first played for Great Britain Mal Reilly sent him a print-out of his performance. How many tackles made, how many missed, how many busts he had done, how many times he had driven it in. Statistics and computer print-outs are a far cry from our days of coming straight from work to play.

☐ When I talk to the lads I know about Rugby they ask daft questions like, 'Do you pull hair or fight?' but when they come to watch a game they realise what a good game we play. My boyfriend played Rugby and trained during the week. I never did anything but wait around for him, then I started playing Rugby. Well, he trained on Tuesday and I trained on Wednesday, he trained on Thursday and I trained on Friday. He played on Saturday and I played on Sunday. I always went to watch him on Saturday but it was rare for him to come and see me play on Sunday.

I liked the Rugby and the social life but he wasn't too happy. He asked me to give up the Rugby - we finished.

☐ They set up a Welsh Sports Hall of Fame. Billy Boston was invited to open it at the County Hall. He told me that he would have given away a lot of what he had achieved in Rugby League for just one Welsh Rugby Union cap. I said, 'Go on then, tell them, tell them all.'

☐ When you look at the conflict between Union and League you are looking at class war. Union is the establishment trying to protect its own with conservative values. Union runs wick like a parasite through schools, the forces, the universities and colleges, the old boys' network and if you're not wearing the right type of tie, you're not in the club.

☐ Joining Hull University was a daunting enough experience for me at eighteen but the Athletic Union Freshers' Bazaar was ten times worse. Everyone wanted us and the beer was their main persuasive weapon. Following several tempting offers my inebriated state led me to the decision that I should join the Rugby Union club, as all good southern public schoolboys do, so you can imagine my shock when I woke up the following day to find I was a member of the University Rugby League club!

My curiosity got the better of me and I decided to find out what this weird perversion of Rugby played by northerners was really like. A couple of training sessions later and I was convinced that this was the game for me. The lads at the club, not all from Rugby League heartland, were very friendly and the game itself seemed to have a great deal of potential.

My enjoyment of the game increased. I was moved from my old Union position on the wing to the half-backs and it was here that I discovered the true strengths of the game: imaginative vision, stamina and sheer guts.

I wanted to put something back into the game so I took on the responsibility of Club Secretary. This thankless but essential job entailed all aspects of matches from arranging and confirming fixtures through to booking pitches, referees and teas.

The satisfaction came in the form of a successful day in which everything went well and I was able to call up Bev Risman, the Student Rugby League Director, with the result of two wins for the Hull University teams.

Rugby League is a microcosm of life where hard graft and determination brings its just rewards, albeit with the help of some ability. My interest continues as a member of the House of Commons Rugby League Group, which is a far cry from being pissed and joining the wrong club!

☐ We went to see Archie Hamilton, Minister for the Armed Forces, a six foot eight inch ex-Guards and public school man. The All-Party delegation included Merlyn Rees, Gary Waller (a Tory MP from Keighley), Tom O'Donovan (the Development Officer) and Maurice Oldroyd from BARLA. We were trying to promote the idea of playing Rugby League in the Forces. He trotted out the usual excuses; 'insurance is difficult, time off is hard to arrange, lack of equipment', and 'anyway, nobody wanted to play it.' We provided evidence that servicemen did and it got to the point where I was glowering at him on the edge of my chair. All we wanted was a level playing field. In the end we struck a deal: if they allowed us to recruit, we would pay the insurance. At that point the civil servants went apoplectic, they told the Minister it couldn't be done. There was no 'Yes, Minister' as is the usual case, but open revolt. We went into the Minister's ante-room under a tense atmosphere. I looked at one of the civil servants and said, 'We'll have a Labour Government soon and when Alan Rogers becomes Defence Minister I hope he sends you serving drinks in the Officers' Mess at Aldershot!'

☐ When I was in the Army they asked me what sports I played. I told them Rugby. One Saturday afternoon I was invited to play. I realised only as we kicked off that they were playing Rugby Union.

☐ The whole system of grant allocations in sport in the Army is based on outmoded ideas which serve the needs and aspirations of officers and not squaddies. You can get Army grants for lacrosse and fencing easier than for Rugby League.

☐ During the days of National Service there was a lot of competition between the RAF and the Army to recruit Rugby League players. As far as they were concerned, as soon as a League player went into the Forces, he went back to amateur status, so there was a rush to get top League professionals to join up.

I got my call-up date, but they asked me to report to Oswestry camp two weeks early so that I could play for Western Command against Northern Command. In Army representative games the match programme told you which were the League players by putting a little asterisk at the side of their name.

I played against all the top club sides - Gloucester, Leicester, Harlequins and Oxford and Cambridge Universities; against the Territorials at Cardiff Arms Park and against the British Police at Bath. It was all a big build-up for the kill at Twickenham. I played four times at Twickenham. The *Daily Telegraph* reported on one game I played there and said a try I scored against the Navy was an even better try than the one scored by Prince Obolensky. They once timed me with a stopwatch while I was still in the Army at 9.8 for one hundred yards.

☐ I completed my journey and education as a referee by taking charge of the Rhine Army final in Detmold, Germany. It was between the Fourth Armoured Workshop - hairy-arsed mechanics - and the Third Light Infantry. The Workshop won a bloody cup three foot tall, bigger than the Challenge Cup. The game was sportingly played between lads who were mostly from Huddersfield and Halifax. There were helicopters taking off and landing and I couldn't hear my whistle at times. The Regimental Sergeant Major who looked after me told me that we couldn't even have got on the field if the Ministry of Defence hadn't given the go ahead. It went right back to the Minister of the Armed Forces. Imagine that, a sports fixture having to be agreed by a top man in the MoD!

☐ People talk a lot about the great referees of the past. People like Sergeant Major Eric Clay. The thing was, people like him never had to go through the mincer of video analysis, with fans, directors and any Tom, Dick and Harry ready to pounce on mistakes. Also they had nowhere near the same standards of fitness. A man called John Thornhill was doing a study on stress in sport at Liverpool University. He strapped a heart testing box with Velcro fastenings to me before a game at St. Helens. When they got the computer spew out they found that my heart-rate went up to 180 per minute when I moved just four feet to give a contentious try. It also said that my heart rate went to the same 180 when I ran 70 yards to award another try. That beggars one question - what would have happened if I'd had to run 70 yards to award a contentious try? We mustn't forget that the powers that be brought in ECG testing after we lost three referees with heart attacks in five years.

☐ I've been to refereeing seminars in Bath, Henley in Arden, Mansfield and Sunderland. At one of our seminars we had a sports psychologist. She drew a circle and enclosed it with an isosceles triangle. At one angle she wrote 'Coach', at another 'Ref' and at the other 'Manager'. Inside the circle she wrote 'Team'. She then asked what could the team in the circle do without and still play. The answer is simple, you can play without a coach or a manager, but not without the ref. Put like that you realise how important the ref is.

The psychologist then asked us to write down things that we thought might make us referee a game badly. Most of the refs put 'being late', 'the wife's been playing hell' and things like that. The psychologist told us we had to put these things in a black box until after the game. I realised that I'd been doing that subconsciously for years. What I'd done by instinct, she proved right. In fact, if I think about it, if the wife had been playing hell with me I used to referee like a trooper. I used to go on the field and think, 'Right! Let them start today!'

I can't say that in thirty years of refereeing I enjoyed the games. I thought about it as a therapy, a deflection or change of direction from the job I did during the week. But when I've thought about the game afterwards while sitting in the bath, I've enjoyed it then.

☐ I got my MBE in 1989. I stood in Buckingham Palace looking at all the murals on the ceiling. All these pictures and a lad from the Eastmoor estate among Colonels with polished boots and Admirals. It was the same time as the King's Cross fire and I can remember thinking, 'How can they give this medal to a sports referee when there's these firemen risking their lives.'

A bloke sidled up in a morning suit. I saw him coming but I didn't get the chance to side step.

'Is t'alright Fred.'

I thought, 'That's a bloody funny accent for in here.'

He turned out to be a Bolton industrialist and he bent my ear for an hour and a half about Wigan. I thought, 'Well ... I've come all this bloody way ...'

☐ A curse on anyone who does harm to this wonderful game. A curse on those who tried to prevent kids playing warm-ups for professional games, a curse on those who want to make Rugby League a national institution at the expense of the small communities in which it flourishes.

☐ The medieval king had his champions - knights who did battle for him. In Fev they have the Rovers players, the big, rough men who don't fight for the nobility, they fight for those who for generations have been disadvantaged up here in the North of England and yet haven't lost their pride. People who are convinced that Fev is the best place on earth. Since there is nothing in Fev that could realistically nourish this belief, this local patriotism is a question of pure faith. And a question of survival. To defend this faith the Rovers go out on the playing field Sunday after Sunday without fail.

On the turf body stands against body, strength against strength, open and unprotected. The players wear no helmets, gloves or pads like the players in American football who look like superheroes from comic strips in their armour. The violence of a Rugby match is not the abstract of the twentieth century, it is concrete, unfiltered and can be experienced at any time during the match. You think that you can feel the collision of bodies as though with your own body.

Pain has to be borne as unnoticed as possible. After the match one of them will sit in the changing room with a dislocated shoulder, his thigh injury with half a dozen stitches from the previous Sunday will have opened up again. He will sit there with a glassy-eyed stare and suffer in silence. Pain and injuries only qualify as topics when they have gone. Past players, hobby players included, will then tap their nose and say proudly, 'Fractured ten times', or they point to impressive scars. Like the council officer who, over a pizza, rips open his shirt and points to the thirty-six stitches with which his shoulder was sewn back on after it had been half torn off during a match.

The logic of pain and violence is different here. After the match players of all teams will say, 'We go out and kick the shit out of them, and with the final whistle we're friends again.' In the meantime, the aggressions have been totally ground away and consumed through two thousand body contacts. So now the knights can change back into decent upstanding citizens of their communities.

What would Fev be without Rugby? Or Cas, or Leigh or anywhere? Small, grey towns that had their day, that were born from coal and died with it, like so many up here in the North. At the end of such sombre thoughts there is always a Sunday when a cheeky scrum-half outflanks three opponents, dives over the line and triumphantly plants the rugby ball on to the ground. That's victory. The fans cheer their champions and their faith will hold fast to the next Seventh Day.

List of Plates

Front cover	When push comes to shove		Page 81	An official gathering at Keighley
Back cover	St. Helens' Kevin Ward enters the fray at Naughton Park		Page 83	Official warning for London Crusader mascot
Page 4	Three hours before the match		Page 85	Reserve official, Odsal Stadium
Page 6	Adam Foggerty brought to ground at Halifax		Page 88	Alex Murphy and Maurice Bamford, Bramley vs Huddersfield
Page 7	Father and son at Hull K.R.		Page 90	Defeat at Wigan for Castleford
Page 8	St. Helens warm up at Fartown		Page 92	Nothing left to give, Huddersfield's narrow win over Keighley
Page 10	Oldham vs Sheffield Eagles		Page 95	Keighley vs Batley
Page 12	Huddersfield bench, Fartown		Page 97	Watching Workington vs Sheffield Eagles
Page 14	Barrow head towards the pitch		Page 98	Queueing up for Castleford vs Widnes
Page 16	Try at Hilton Park, Leigh		Page 99	Halifax head for the pitch, Thrum Hall
Page 18	Reserve official, Bramley		Page 101	Workington skyline
Page 21	All the family, Castleford		Page 106	Half-time at The Willows, Salford
Page 24	Roy Powell off-loads the ball against Wigan		Page 108	Batley fan, Doncaster fan
Page 25	Legs eleven, Wigan vs Keighley		Page 111	Castleford bench
Page 27	On the way to Post Office Road, Featherstone		Page 113	Having a shave, Workington
Page 29	Substituted player takes in liquid, Wheldon Road		Page 115	Fly like an eagle
Page 30	Television man		Page 116	Barrow score box
Page 32	'No way, Ref!' Castleford vs Widnes		Page 120	Headingley crowd
Page 34	Pre-match game of dominoes, Social Club, Headingley		Page 121	Baby at Keighley
Page 35	Rugby League Headquarters, Chapeltown Road, Leeds		Page 122	Waiting for a lift, Thrum Hall
Page 38	Try at Wilderspool		Page 128	Getting to grips with St. Helens
Page 39	Shouting on the team, Leeds vs Featherstone		Page 132	Winning try, Wakefield vs Wigan
Page 42	Widnes vs St. Helens		Page 133	Old man at Wheldon Road
Page 43	Halifax fan vs Bradford Northern, Thrum Hall		Page 136	Physiotherapy room, Workington
Page 48	Injured player at Batley		Page 137	Oldham player and supporter, Watersheddings
Page 50	Concussed at Wilderspool, Warrington vs Hull K.R.		Page 140	Searching for the right tune, Fartown
Page 51	St. John's Ambulance at Belle Vue, Wakefield		Page 141	Waiting for half-time at Headingley
Page 52	Half-time drink at Fartown		Page 144	Mushy peas at Wheldon Road
Page 54	Glorious mud, Leigh vs Leeds		Page 146	Half-time raffle, Keighley
Page 55	'It sometimes needs three washes.' Central Park, Wigan		Page 147	Fan leaving early
Page 56	Owen Simpson post-match, Oldham		Page 150	Ice-bag on thigh, Whitehaven
Page 60	End of match, Leigh vs London Crusaders		Page 151	Steve Gibson, Salford vs Hull
Page 61	Smile please, Henderson		Page 153	Cheerleaders, Bradford Northern vs Salford
Page 63	Family fan club, Keighley vs Batley		Page 154	Wakefield Panthers vs Redhill in Cup Final
Page 64	Wigan at Wembley		Page 155	Front row, Castleford
Page 66	Wigan on the road again		Page 158	Huddersfield kit man
Page 69	Wigan try at Wembley		Page 160	End of match, Doncaster
Page 71	Batley banter		Page 164	Time keepers, Whitehaven vs Huddersfield
Page 72	A try for Leigh		Page 165	Penalty at Post Office Road
Page 73	Celebration time at Wilderspool		Page 168	Missed opportunity at Belle Vue
Page 76	Waiting for a conversion, Featherstone vs St. Helens		Page 169	Caught short pre-match, Post Office Road
Page 79	Referee John Holdsworth warms up under Wigan's stand		Page 170	St. Helens ' Kevin Ward enters the fray at Naughton Park

We would like to thank the following people who subscribed to this book:

Fred Bailey, Hemsworth
Rachel Redman, Pontefract
Richard Brown, Castleford
Steve Hobson, Wakefield
H. George, Snaith
Ian Dransfield, Featherstone
Tony&WendySpurr, Huddersfield
George Gott, Pontefract
Nicola Adams, Castleford
Paul Schofield, Pontefract
Edgar Thrall, Pontefract
Lee F. Carson, Wakefield
Graham Williams, Leeds
Edward A. Domville, Warrington
Patrick Bondy, Harlow
Tony Ackroyd, Halifax
D. N. Wike, Blackburn
M. A. Taylor, Wakefield
Peter A. Moir, Rickmanworth
D. A. Mitchell, Leeds
Andrew Bates, Wigan
Andy Gladwin, Brixton
Stephen Hartshorne, Wakefield
Geoffrey Moorhouse, Hawes
E. E. Day, Warrington
William Rolfe, Oldham
Mark Gillespie, Castleford
Paul Robert Sephton, Preston
Stan Allen, Birmingham
T. Casey, Bolton
Stephen P. Boothroyd, Leeds
Craig Henny, Halifax
Dale Else, Wakefield
T. M. Driver, Keighley
R. M. Pearson, Bradford
R. B. Austin, Knaresborough
Bill G. Lythgoe, Wigan
Patricia Arthur, Birkenhead
J. Pollard, Leeds
Steve Lawrence, Salford
B. Coen, Leeds
Gerald McLoughlen, Wigan

F. Birchall, Manchester
M. Turner, Chorley
Stephen J. Gleeson, Holland
K. G. Royston, Featherstone
M. Kelly, Northwich
Michael McCauley, St Helens
Keith G. Thompson, Wakefield
W. J. Bullough, Wakefield
J. Neill Tunnicliffe, Ealing
Caroline Hutchinson, Featherstone
Graeme Smith, Liversedge
Ian Jackson, Manchester
Geoff W. Ellis, Stockport
Terry Kirk, Pontefract
D. A. Dickson, Stockport
P. G. Bradbury, Manchester
Brian Collett, Bradford
Adrian J. McGuire, Keighley
S. A. Cannon, Bradford
G. Jumps, Hull
Jack Addison, Featherstone
Alan Walker, Wakefield
Bill Nelson, Cleator Moor
B. Dixon, Hull
J. E. Irving, Carlisle
Robert Clarke, Hull
S. Fitton, Bridlington.
Michael Jackson, Leeds
Phill Brown, Skelmersdale
Geoff Lee, Bradford
Hugh Robinson, Bradford
Helen B. Bullock, Wakefield
Anthony Holstead, Killinghall
E. L. Farrar, Pontefract
S. G. Bonnerman, Milnrow
'The Rugby League Supporters
Association', Leeds
Malcolm Ferguson, Durham
Iain Rowland, London
M. Smith, Pontefract
David Bruce, Salford
T. Nelthorpe, Stockport

Phil Brown, Wigan
Steven Hepworth, Germany
Kathleen Sexton, Hull
Alison Hewitt, Wetherby
M. Brown, Hull
Peter Elliot, Wakefield
John S. Edwards, Manchester
T. A. Cook, Loughton
A. J. Spicer, Wrawby
Stephen R. Davies, Southport
Steven Dean, St-Leonards-on-Sea
Geoffrey Cook, Oldham
Andrew England, Huddersfield
Brian Platt, Batley
Ian Ward, Oldham
Darren Gill, Wakefield
D. M. Houghton, Wigan
J. B. Sykes, Wigan
B. Rowlin, Hull
S. M. Batty, Hull
Guy Smith, Huddersfield
C. A. Lomas, Manchester
Brian Saxton, Hemsworth
Ian Williams, Colchester
Deborah J. Daniels, Wigan
Joseph S. Pledger, Wigan
Roger Young, Bristol
P.W. Reed, Oxon
Jill Flanagan, Normanton
Nick & Amanda Evans, Germany
John C. Brown, Birmingham
Jim Walker, Walsall
A. R. Wallis, Castleford
Roger Green, Pontefract
Donald Hunt, Pontefract
R.H. Terretta, Runcorn
Martin Oxley, Featherstone
Trevor Wainwright, Castleford
Geoffrey Lofthouse M.P., Pontefract
T. Keaveney M.B.E., Huddersfield
R. L. Thomas, Oldham
Melanie Mays, Rotherham

Mick Griffiths, Wakefield
John Etty, Fleetwood
Robert E. Gate, Sowerby Bridge
Brenda Dobek, Leeds
Colin Dennis, Sheffield
Brian Lewis, Pontefract
Geoffrey Bullock, Wakefield .
A. J. Lockwood, Pontefract
Jackie Wilkinson, Castleford
Terry Wynn, St Helens
Tony Lumb, Featherstone
Steve Wagner, Featherstone
Trevor Griffiths, Wetherby
K. A. McCarrick, Wigan
Charles Davison, Castleford
Nick Woolf, Pinner
David Thompson, Australia
Len Garbett, Castleford
Rachel Van Riel, Pontefract
Trevor Delaney, Keighley
Robert Jolley, Pontefract
Ruth Beck, Sheffield
Richard Clarkson, Wakefield
Ray Connolly, Thornton-Cleveleys
Jim Dickinson, Featherstone
K. S. Davenport, Widnes
Gordon Tegg, Oxted
John J. Morris, Liverpool
Stephen Morris, Wakefield
Ron Dredge, Knaresborough
Ian Proctor, Leeds
Lynn Taylor, Featherstone
Peter Birchall, Rochdale
Reginald Jukes, Pontefract
Maureen Williams, Featherstone
Ian Daley, Featherstone
Isabel Galan, Manchester
Amanda Lovell, Castleford
Andrew Lovell, Castleford
David Goldthorp, Hull
The Rock Inn, Glasshoughton
John Windeatt, Glasshoughton

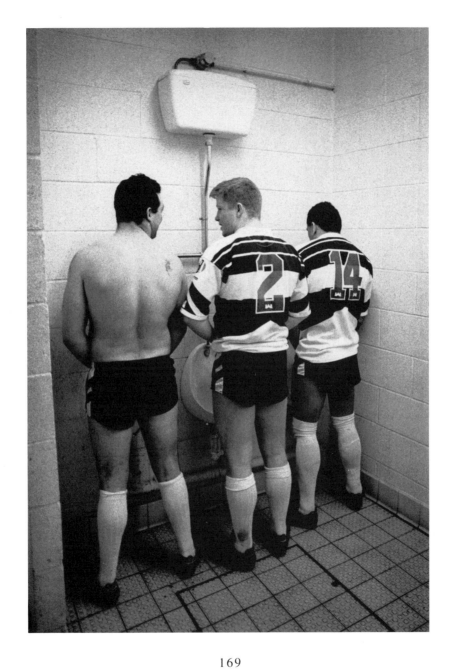